TOPICS

OF

JURISPRUDENCE

CONNECTED WITH

CONDITIONS

OF

FREEDOM AND BONDAGE.

BY

JOHN C. HURD,

COUNSELLOR AT LAW.

NEW YORK:
D. VAN NOSTRAND, 192 BROADWAY.
M.DCCC.LVI.

ENTERED according to Act of Congress, in the year 1856, by
JOHN CODMAN HURD,
In the Clerk's Office of the District Court of the United States, for the Southern District of New York.

JOHN F. TROW,
STEREOTYPER AND ELECTROTYPER,
879 Broadway.

ADVERTISEMENT.

It is not probable that readers will be found for these pages unless among two classes of persons. One being those who by constitution of mind, and previous studies, are inclined to that branch of speculation which Chancellor D'Aguesseau, in the first volume of his works, (page 449,) calls the metaphysics of jurisprudence, and recommends as a preliminary study for the practical lawyer. There cannot in any country be many whose studies have taken this direction. Such persons are not numerous even in the ranks of the professors and practitioners of legal science. And it would only be in accordance with the prevailing assertions of the tendency of the minds of Americans to subjects of immediately practical use, to say that such persons are more rarely to be found in this, than in some other countries, of a corresponding degree of intellectual culture. However, whether this is so or not, there are some reasons for believing that the systematic exposition of the elementary principles of legal science is likely to receive increased attention in England and America. It is hoped that some of those whose inquiries have been directed to this subject, may find an interest in the attempt made in these two chapters to state in a consistent form some of the most elementary and abstract principles of jurisprudence, and that the citations given may serve to make more known the works of some European authors, which will be found valuable aids in pursuing this branch of study.

The other class of persons, among whom it is hoped some will be found to take an interest in the subject of these chapters, is certainly far more numerous:—those who wish to examine those legal questions, arising out of the existence of domestic slavery in some of the States of the American Union, which may affect the rights and obligations of the inhabitants of the other States. The importance of these questions at the present time it is unnecessary to enlarge upon. In the following pages it is attempted to state only the most elementary and abstract principles necessary to be established in making a legal examination of the questions, so far as it is possible to do so without making any reference to the fundamental principles of law peculiar to this country. The attempt thus to state, by themselves, and apart from any illustration by actual cases, a connected system of abstract principles of law applicable to a subject of practical importance, is certainly attended with some difficulty. A discussion, however, which should not be based on some principles admitted by all who may take part in it, would be a logical absurdity; and whatever may be the success of the effort here made in that direction, it cannot but be admitted to be a reasonable endeavor.

Some of the practical questions whose solution is connected with the accurate determination of the principles indicated in these chapters, will suggest themselves to every reader. And although it is herein intended only to state principles, and ascertain some general rules, without applying them to any of the questions now before the American public, it may give an interest to such abstract discussion to suggest some of those questions to whose examination these inquiries are supposed to be preliminary. The two chapters here offered being intended to be introductory to the consideration of such questions in a treatise, which may be entitled, *A View of the Laws of Freedom and Bondage in the United States*, the contents of the chapters under which the subject will be distributed will, therefore, be here briefly described. It being premised that the view taken will be a purely *legal* one, that is, entirely distinct from all ethical and political considerations. The two chapters here given will constitute an Elementary, or General Part. The six chapters next following form a Historical Part. Of these, three (Ch. III., IV., V.) will relate to the establishment of municipal, or national law, in the English colonies of America, under the following distribution :—

CHAPTER III.—Of the common law of England taking effect in the colonies as a personal law, according to principles set forth in the first two chapters, and of the location of political power under the public law of the Empire, by which an alteration of the private law might take place.

CHAPTER IV.—Of principles of universal jurisprudence, or the *law of nations*, relating to conditions of freedom or of bondage, which, in accordance with the doctrines of the same chapters, may be taken to have formed part of the common law of England. Since, according to these doctrines, a rule of universal jurisprudence must be proved from an extended view of the laws of many nations, this will involve an examination of the Roman law on this subject, and a more particular inquiry into the position which it occupies in connection with the national law of any one country, than is given in the first and second chapters. And, it being supposed that the *law of nations* is not necessarily the same at all times, its recognition in the law of England will be traced, after the first settlement of the colonies, to the time of their political separation from Great Britain, concluding with an examination of the doctrines of Lord Mansfield in Somerset's case, operating as part of the local, or *inter-*

nal law of England. The same doctrines, in connection with the private *international* law of the British Empire, will be further noticed in the seventh chapter.

CHAPTER V.—Of the effect of the *law of nations*, and of English statute law, in establishing slavery in the colonies.

The next two chapters (VI., VII.) will pursue the history of the local law of the colonies relating to freedom and its opposites.

CHAPTER VI.—Containing a chronological abstract of the legislative action of each of the local colonial governments in America, affecting personal rights. This legislation may be either internal or international in its operation, or extent; and so far as it is of the latter character, it will be connected with the subject of

CHAPTER VII.—Which relates to the private international law of the colonies and the British Empire during the period of their union with it; including a further notice of Somerset's case in this connection; and also an examination of principles of the common law of the Empire, affecting the extradition of criminals, as between its several jurisdictions, and in relation to demands of foreign states. The purpose being to ascertain whether the liberties of private persons in such cases were determined by the *administrative* or the *judicial* function of government.

CHAPTER VIII.—Is included in the Historical Part, in being descriptive of the political change in the location of sovereign power which occurred between the commencement of the Revolution to the final establishment of the present Constitution of the United States. The same chapter belongs, also, to the third division of the subject, which may be called the Practical Part, in presenting a view of doctrines of public law, which determine the investiture of sovereign political power over persons and things in the territorial domain occupied by the United States—meaning both States and Territories.

CHAPTER IX.—A general view of the incidents of conditions of freedom and its opposites, in reference to the public law of the United States. This will comprise an examination of the constitutional test of political power; of the possible application of sovereign power in producing law, which is either internal or international according to its personal and territorial extent. By following out these distinctions, the remainder of the subject will be considered as either internal private law, or international private law, as follows:—

CHAPTER X.—The national municipal (internal) law of the United States—that is, the law operating in the United States as one national dominion—in its effects on conditions of freedom and bondage.

CHAPTER XI.—The municipal (internal) law of the several jurisdictions constituting the United States, both States and Territories. This will be in the form of a chronological view of the legislative acts having this operation, or extent, as they relate to the subject, being, in a historical point of view, a continuation of the sixth chapter. The objects of legislation being necessarily only indicated, in most instances; statutes being more or less fully described, according to their bearing on the subjects of the succeeding chapters; particularly those which are international in their operation: the remaining chapters relating to the private international law of the United States relating to conditions of freedom, &c.

CHAPTER XII.—A general view of the existence and operation of private international law in the United States, distinguishing, 1st, a *quasi*-international law—a law having an international operation, but identified in authority with the national municipal law, i. e., the law of the United States as one nation, or state; and, 2d, an international private law, properly so called—a law operating in the several local districts of the United States—States and Territories—as political jurisdictions reciprocally independent.

The first of these will form the subject of eleven chapters, XIII. to XXIV.

CHAPTER XIII.—General view of the Fourth Article of the Constitution of the United States as that from which only the *quasi*-international law, above described, can derive its existence.

CHAPTER XIV.—A few remarks on the first section of this Article in connection with the general subject.

CHAPTER XV.—The first paragraph of the second section of this Article in the same connection—examination of the extent of the terms, "the citizens of each State."

CHAPTER XVI.—Further examination of the same clause: effect of the words, "the privileges and immunities of citizens."

CHAPTERS XVII. to XXIII. will relate to the second and third paragraphs of the second section of the Fourth Article.

CHAPTER XVII.—Of the persons who may be demanded, or claimed, under the second and third paragraphs, as fugitives from justice, or from labor.

CHAPTER XVIII.—Of the manner in which these two provisions take effect upon private persons. Here the question of the proper construction of these clauses, or their character as either public or private international law, will be examined.

Five chapters, XIX. to XXIII., will relate to the means by which these provisions may be carried into effect.

CHAPTER XIX.—Examination whether, construing the provision relating to fugitives from service, or labor, as private law, it executes itself in any sense—whether the fugitive may be seized independently of the action of any public authority.

CHAPTER XX.—Examination whether, on the supposition that either of these two provisions may be carried into effect by the government of the United States, there are any other provisions in the Constitution which must regulate the exercise of its power.

CHAPTER XXI.—Examination whether Congress has power to legislate in respect to the execution of these provisions.

CHAPTER XXII.—On the supposition of a power in Congress to legislate, examination whether the means provided by the actual legislation for the delivery of fugitives from justice *are necessary and proper*.

CHAPTER XXIII.—The same inquiry in respect to the legislation of Congress relating to fugitives from labor.

The preceding chapters on the effect of the constitutional provisions are classed under *quasi*-international law.

CHAPTER XXIV.—Relates to private international law, properly so called, operating between the States as independent political districts—being identified in each with the local, municipal, or internal law of such several jurisdiction. The propriety of the classification of the cases arranged under that head will, of course, depend on the extent of the constitutional provisions. This division of the private international law being taken to apply in cases not coming under the clauses of the Fourth Article.

CHAPTER XXV.—Will relate to private international law of the United States as one nation, or state, affecting the relations of persons coming from foreign states, and the relations of domiciled inhabitants of the United States as affected by the laws of foreign countries.

NEW YORK, *August*, 1856.

TOPICS OF JURISPRUDENCE

CONNECTED WITH

CONDITIONS OF FREEDOM AND BONDAGE.

CHAPTER I.

LAW DEFINED AND DIVIDED—ITS OBJECT, ORIGIN, EFFECT, AND EXTENT.

§ 1. The word *law* has, in common use, two leading significations; one, which is generally considered the *primary* sense —that of a *rule of action*, prescribed by a superior to an inferior; in the idea of which the possibility of action contrary to the rule is implied: the other—a meaning sometimes considered *secondary* to that first given, by a metaphorical use of the word—that of a mode of existence, or of action, excluding the idea of the possibility of action contrary to that mode;—a relation necessary in the nature of the thing existing or acting: whether the co-existence of a superior author or cause of that relation be supposed or not.[1]

§ 2. Every being, existing under conditions over which it has no control, is subject to law in the secondary sense;—therefore, called the law of its nature. The nature of man, or the conditions of his existence, are to him a law in this sense—the law of nature; and, being by this law capable of choice and action, he may also be subject to law in the primary sense.[2]

---

[1] Brande's Dict., *Law*. Blackst. Com., Introd., sec. 2, note by Christian. Austin: Province of Jurisp., pp. 19, 130, 184. Montesq.: Spirit of L., ch. i.; and De Tracy's Comment. Reddie's Inquiries Elementary &c., pp. 4, 16, 17.

[2] The primary and secondary *meanings* of the *term* law must not be confounded

The idea of law in the primary sense implies the relation of superior and inferior ; and the elementary principle in the *science* of law, in this sense of the word *law*, is the existence of the legislator anterior to the law. When the word *law* is applied to rules of action for man, the existence of such a legislator, as to man, must be taken for a fact, or relation, independent of the rule itself; or as being a principle of the *law* of nature, in the secondary sense of the word *law*.[1]

§ 3. In the various views of the conditions of man's existence—that is, of the law of his nature (law in the secondary sense), which have been advanced by authors who have professed to treat of *jurisprudence*, or the *science of law*, there have been two theories as to the existence of this legislator, or the source of law in the primary sense. According to some authors, the first principle of the science of law is, that man exists in society organized into political states, and that the state is the highest source of *law* as a *rule of action*.[2] This principle being assumed to be a *law* of nature, in the secondary sense of the term, and the law of nature, in this sense, being considered as the only law of nature which can, in any system of *jurisprudence*, be regarded as having an existence independent of the state.[3]

According to others, there is a law in the primary sense, anterior to the legislation of the state; by which actions are

with a primary and secondary law ; whether so called in reference to order of time or of authority. Conditions of things are necessarily presupposed in the enunciation of a rule of action, and in this connection the former may be called the primary and the latter the secondary law. Some elementary writers speak of a primary and secondary law of nature. Their primary law being a condition of things—a law in the secondary sense : *e. g.* Bowyer: Univ. Pub. Law, p. 20. Ayliffe's Pandects, pp. 5, 6. Wood's Civil Law, p. 92. Domat: Loix Civ. Traité des Loix, ch. i, § 3.

[1] Reddie's Inq. Elem. &c., p. 16–19.

[2] In illustrating the assertion of this doctrine, writers on jurisprudence usually cite Carneades, *apud* Lactantium, Lib. v., c. 15; and Aristippus and Pyrrho, *apud* Diog. Laert., Lib. ii., c. 8: see Selden, De J. Nat. et Gen. juxta Disc. Eb., ch. 3; Rutherf., B. ii., c. 1 ; Pufend., B. ii., c. 3; Grot., B. et P. Proleg. 5. But these are only early dogmatisms on one side of a never-ending ethical controversy ; of which more systematic assertions might be found nearer our own day. It is not, in fact, possible to cite any system of jurisprudence or any legislative or juridical authority, ancient or modern, heathen or Christian, which denies the pre-existence of natural justice—the jural character of every rule which is a rule of law ; unless piratical communities and robber feudal barons can be called juridical authority when denying the existence of any law : compare Lieber : Pol. Ethics, vol. i, 231.

[3] Spinoza : Ethices, Pars iv., prop. 37, schol. 2 : Tract. Politici, cap. ii. : Tract. Theologico-Polit., cap. xvi. Hobbes is commonly misrepresented as having denied the existence of natural law otherwise than in this sense.

enjoined, allowed or prohibited, independently of the rule proceeding from the state, and under which, as a law of nature, and a law in the primary sense also, the state is to be considered as existing; which law is to be recognized in jurisprudence as constantly binding on mankind.[1]

§ 4. The questions of the *existence* of natural law,—in the primary sense of the word *law*, of the nature of its injunctions, and of the limits of the power of the state as a source of rules of action for mankind, are questions regarding the nature of man, or of the *law* of his nature, in the *secondary* sense of the term *law:* they are questions of *ethics*,—the science of his nature as a being capable of choice and action in reference to a rule which it is possible for him to disobey; whether they are determined by the precepts of a religious creed, taken to be the revelation of a divine will, or by the dictates of human reason. Whether they also belong to *jurisprudence*, or not, is merely a question of definition: that is, depends on the meaning of *law*, and of *jurisprudence* as the science of law.[2]

§ 5. A law in the secondary sense is spoken of as something which exists absolutely; which necessarily both exists and operates; which is necessarily enforced, if it exists at all; such a law being a *state of things*. But a law in the primary sense—a rule of action, may be supposed to exist without being enforced; or without operating except in creating a moral obligation: because a possibility of action contrary to the rule is implied in the idea of a law in this sense. A law of this kind may therefore be recognized either as a law merely existing, or as a law operating or being enforced.

Now, jurisprudence is taken to be the science of a rule not merely existing, but one which is actually operative or enforced

---

[1] Lieber: Pol. Ethics, B. I., § 30. Rutherford, B. ii., c. 2. Mackintosh: Prog. Eth. Phil., Sect. iv. v.: Grotius: B. et P. Prolegom., §§ 6, 7, 8, 16, and notes. Vattel: c. ii., § 1. Aristot.: Rhet., Lib. i., cap. 13 et 15, and various other ancient authorities cited by Selden, De J. Nat. &c., Ebr. Lib. i., ch. vi. Reddie's Inquiries &c., p. 19; also, ch. ii., and the citations.

A very recent comparison of the best authors on this point in Bowyer on Universal Public Law, ch. ii., iii., iv., vii., Vol. 84, of Philad. Law Library.

[2] Comp., Doctor and Student, ch. i., ii.

In connection with the subject of this chapter, there will be frequent occasion to recall the maxim of Iavolenus, Dig., Lib. l., Tit. 17, § 202. Omnis definitio in jure civili periculosa est, parum est enim ut non subverti possit.

in or by the will of society or the state. The science of what rule *ought* to be made operative by the will of the state is a different thing; it is a science of rules regarded only as existing, whether operative in civil society—that is, enforced—or not.[1]

A rule made operative by the authority of society, or of the state, is a rule identified with the expressed will of society or of the state. The will of the state, indicated in some form of expression, is *the law*,† the subject of *jurisprudence*, and no natural rule which may exist, forms a part of *the law* unless identified with the will of the state so indicated. What the state wills is the conterminous measure of law; no pre-existing rule is the measure of that will.[2]

§ 6. But a law in the *primary* sense must be founded on a recognition of the nature of the things which it affects:—that is, of a natural *law* in the secondary sense of the word: for a rule founded on a contradiction of the nature of things is a rule impossible to be executed, or cannot subsist as a rule.[4] Therefore, all laws made for man must recognize some conditions as the conditions of his existence; and hence a recognition of his moral nature, or of a necessity in his nature to regard actions as

---

[1] Domat includes natural law, derived by *a priori* reasoning, in *the law*—the subject of jurisprudence; and speaks of some rules as being evident without reasoning, and of others which require reasoning to make them evident. Domat: Civil Law. Treatise on Laws, ch. ii., §1—37; and see Bowyer, Univ. Pub. Law, p. 103. In this system, the mind of the individual jurist determines the law; it is his *subjective* apprehension of a rule of action: and only that rule which, in his judgment, the state *ought* to enforce. Chanc. D'Aguesseau approves of Domat's system in this respect: see Œuvres, Tom. I., p. 645–6. Mr. Reddie, Inquiries El. &c., p. 48, says of Kant's Metaphysische Anfangs Gründe der Rechtslehre, and Fichte's Grundlage des Naturrechts, that "they established in Germany the complete recognition of the distinction between ethics and law, or jurisprudence, between the legality and the morality of human actions." But Mr. Reddie sometimes speaks of jurisprudence as if it comprehended the science of what ought to be law; see Inquiries El. &c., pp. 24, 25.

[2] Savigny: Heut. Rom. Recht, § 7. *Tr.*: "With reference to this quality of the law, by which it has an actual determined existence in reference to any given state of things in which it may be appealed to, we call it positive law."

[3] Molloy de Jure Marit. B. iii., c. 9, § 1, 2. Pufendorf, B. i., c. 6, § 1. Co. Litt. fo. 97, b. Lieber: Pol. Eth., vol. I. p. 98, 249. "Law is the direct or indirect, explicit or implied, real or supposed, positive or acquiesced in expression of the will of human society represented in the state; or it is the public will of a part of human society constituted into a state." Compare Encyc. Am., vol. vii., Append. Law, &c., by Judge Story.

[4] Dig. Lib. l., Tit. 17, § 186. Quæ rerum natura prohibentur nulla lege confirmata sunt. Co. Lit., 92 a. "Lex spectat naturæ ordinem, the law respecteth the order and course of nature. Lex non cogit ad impossibilia. The law compels no man to impossible things. The argument *ab impossibili* is forcible in law. Impossibile est quod naturæ rei repugnat."

LAW—A RULE OF RIGHT. 5

being right or wrong, is necessarily made, as the recognition of a fact, in the act of prescribing a law for him founded on the idea of distinguishing between actions as right or wrong, or on the existence of a moral obligation in the rule; that is, an obligation founded on his *nature*, and also resulting from a law in the primary sense.[1] Now, since, in point of fact, all laws, enjoined by society or the state, have been founded on this idea, the law prescribed by the state recognizes the existence of a natural law in the *primary* sense of the word *law*.[2]

§ 7. But since the state makes this acknowledgment of natural law by classifying or distinguishing certain actions as actions to be done or not to be done, as permissible or not permissible,[3] it so far interprets this law of nature by asserting it

---

[1] Whewell: Elements of Morality, including Polity, B. i., c. 4, 90. "Rights are not law only nor justice only, (meaning by law the law of society, and by justice that which is right,) they are both Law and Justice; Law, because Justice; Justice expressed in Law;" and see the same, §§ 105, 106, 107. Lieber: Pol. Eth., B. ii., § 31. "The state, I said, is founded on the relations of right; it is a *jural* society, as a church is a religious society, an insurance company a financial association; the idea of the just, and the action founded upon the idea called justice, is the broad foundation and great object of the state." The same, §§ 33, 35: "The state being a jural society, and rights being imaginable between moral beings only, it follows that the state has likewise a moral character, and must maintain it." The word *jural* is also employed by Whewell, B. i., c. 4, 90: "By the adjective *jural* we shall denote that which has reference to the doctrine of rights and obligations; as by the adjective *moral* we denote that which has reference to the doctrine of duties." And therefore, the state, in establishing coercive rules of action, acts *juridically*. The term *juridical* is commonly used as if synonymous with *judicial*. A tribunal in acting judicially, necessarily, also acts juridically: that is, declares what is justice or right. But the state, when it promulgates laws, promulgates them as rules of right. The word juridical will herein be employed to designate the declaration of *law*, whether made by the legislative or the judicial function.

The term *juridical* is sometimes used to designate the province of the private jurist: the proper word for which is *juristical*, (*Ger*. juristisch.) A society of jurists in England have called themselves "the juridical society." In the French version of Falck's Juristische Encyclopedie, translated Ency. *Juridique*, vii., note, it is said: "nous avons ordinairement traduit l'adjectif allemand *juristisch* par *juridique*, quoique le mot français signifie, dans l'usage plutôt ce qui se rapporte à la *juridiction* que ce qui se rapporte au *droit*. Nous aurions pu souvent le remplacer par *légal*, mais comme il est nécessaire, surtout dans un exposé de principes, de ne pas confondre le *droit* et la *loi*, nous avons évité d'employer l'un pour l'autre, *juridique* (repondant à *juristisch*, *rechtlich*) et *légal* (repondant à *gesetzlich*.)"

[2] Reddie's Inquiries Elem. &c., p. 9, 58. There are noble passages in the writings of Cicero, and others, which are frequently cited by authors who base *jurisprudence* upon *natural law*; (e. g. Cic. De Rep. iii., 22—the passage given by Lactantius, Inst. vi., 8; Demosthenes Or. contra Aristogit. i.) Whether they have been used to the purpose depends entirely on the definitions assumed for these words. Their force differs essentially as they are used either in a legislative or a judicial point of view.

[3] Hobbes: Leviathan, De Civitate, c. xxvi. De legibus civilibus. "Legem igitur civilem sic definio: lex civilis unicuique civi est regula qua civitas verbo scripto, vel alio quocunque voluntatis signo idoneo, ad distinctionem boni et mali uti imperat."

Ency. Am., vol. vii., p. 581. Appendix by Judge Story: "By a law we understand

to be accordant with those distinctions.¹ The maintenance of those distinctions being, therefore, the will of the state, those whom it appoints to carry out its will are bound, from their relations to the state, to accept and enforce those distinctions, as the criterion of the law of nature. Judicial tribunals constituted by the state, must, therefore, in interpreting *the law*, receive these distinctions as the exposition of the law of nature, and as the highest rule to which they can refer. The natural law is included in *the law*, in this ordinary sense, only so far as *the law* is the judgment of the state upon what shall constitute right or wrong action; and it is immaterial, for the judgment of the subordinate tribunals, whether the jurisprudence which they have to interpret is considered to admit, in theory, the existence of natural law, or to refer all rules of action to the authority of the state; since, supposing it to admit the pre-existence of natural law, as a rule of action, it assumes the interpretation of it, given by the state, to be the guide for legal decision.²

a rule prescribed by the sovereign power of a state to its citizens or subjects, declaring some right, enforcing some duty, or prohibiting some act."

¹ This recognition of moral obligation in jurisprudence is entirely independent of the foundation of that obligation, as a question of Ethical Philosophy. It is immaterial in jurisprudence whether the law of nature is called "moral sense; common sense; understanding; rule of right; natural justice; natural equity or good order; truth; doctrine of election; repugnancy to nature," or any such term. Bentham, in quoting these various denominations of the law of nature, asserts the propriety of his own favorite term, "the law of utility," or "greatest happiness principle:" which is equally vague, as the description of a rule of action, until some legislator is assumed to exist, who shall determine what is *useful*, or what is the *greatest happiness*. See Bentham's Morals and Legislation, ch. ii., 14, note. And compare Austin: Prov. Jurisp., p. 133; note, p. 174; Austin being of the same ethical school. Also, Reddie's Inquiries Elem. &c., 2d ed., p. 54—72. Utility has, in fact, always been recognized in juridical action as an exponent of what the law ought to be. See the same, p. 73; and that there is herein no real inconsistency, see Mackintosh: Progress of Ethical Philosophy.

² 2 Dodson's Adm. Rep., The Le Louis, 247. Speaking of the slave-trade, Lord Stowell says: "I must remember that, in discussing this question, I must consider it, not according to any private moral apprehensions of my own, (if I entertained them ever so sincerely,) but as *the law* considers it." ... (p. 249): "An act must be legally criminal—I say *legally* criminal because neither this court nor any other can carry its private apprehensions, independent of law, into its public judgments on the quality of actions. It must conform to the judgment of the law upon that subject; and acting as a court in the administration of law, it cannot impute criminality to an act where the law imputes none. It must look to the legal standard of morality."

Hobbes: Leviath., c. 26—"Leges naturæ et leges civiles in eadem civitate se mutuo continent." Massé Droit Commer., Tom. i., 42. Scaccia Tractat. de Commer. Quæst., VII., Par. ii., Ampl. 19, § 4, 19. Hegel, Grundlinien der Philosophie des Rechts,

§ 8. Since the power of the state, or of society, is assumed by the state to be the result of natural law in the signification either of a necessary condition or of a rule, the only natural principles, which the *law* can recognize as such, are those which admit the existence of society, as natural; and no principles can form a part of it which are founded upon a supposed state of nature, anterior or opposed to society, or on the supposed law of such a state, as being the true law of nature.[1]

§ 9. The actual conditions of human existence have divided mankind into separate communities or states, each called *sovereign*, because each exercises, independently of the rest, those powers of society which are essential to the purposes of such separate existence.[2]

The rules of action prescribed by any single sovereignty or state are known to the individuals under its dominion as the *law*, in the ordinary sense (in contradistinction to ethics); or *national* law (commonly termed in English, municipal),[3] as

§ 212 : "Im positiven Rechte ist daher das was gesetzmässig ist, die Quelle der Erkentniss dessen was *Recht* ist, oder eigentlich, was Rechtens ist : "—
This proposition is almost untranslatable from the want of an English word corresponding with the German *Recht*, Latin *Jus*, French *droit*. Law being used not to designate that only but what is meant by the Ger. *Gesezt*, Lat. *lex*, Fr. *loi*. (Lieber's Pol. Eth., sect. 30, n.). The passage is equivalent to:—In law—the rule identified with the will of the state, that which is legal, or according to law, (*lex, loi, Gesetz,*) is the means of ascertaining that which is the rule of right—the *jural* rule, *jus, droit, Recht* :—and not *vice versa*.
The American Literature on the Slavery question affords numberless instances, in which the converse of this proposition is made the foundation of the argument.

[1] Spinoza : Tractatus Politici, cap. ii., 15. Domat : Loix Civ. Tr., ch. ii., § 2. Cousin : Introd. Hist. Philo., p. 11 : " In the place of primitive society, where all things were in confusion, man created a new society upon the basis of one single idea, that of justice. Justice established constitutes the state. The use of the state is to cause justice to be respected by means of force. * * * Hence arises a new state of society, civil and political society, which is nothing less than justice acting by means of that legal order which the state represents."
Professor Foster's Introductory Lecture before the London University. Law Magazine, N. Y., Feb. 1852. "If asked, therefore, to explain the expression employed at the outset—natural law,—the answer would be, that portion of moral obligation which is enforceable by public authority." Comte : Tr. de Legislation, Liv. i., ch. 6. Compare Calhoun, A Disquisition on Government ; Works, vol. i., p. 58.

[2] A fact assumed in every system of jurisprudence. Comp. Lieber : Pol. Eth., B. ii., § 61. Bla. Com., vol. i., Introd., p. 42.

[3] This portion of the subject of jurisprudence is ordinarily denominated *municipal* law by English writers. Blackstone (Comm. I., Introd., p. 44) is most commonly cited as authority for its use : but it was employed by English lawyers long before his time, (see I. Vaughan, R. 191, anno 17, Car. ii.,) to signify the law of any one state or nation ; or, what is commonly called " the law of the land." According to the analogy of the languages of Continental Europe *municipal law* would imply the local law of some political body less than a state or nation—the law of a *municipium*, a town or

proceeding from the authority of a single polity or state, and having effect only within the territorial limits of its dominion. These rules may or may not be consistent with the law of nature, or true principles of ethics, but in being prescribed by the highest power within the limits of such state, and constituting the judgment of such power on the principles and effect of natural law, they must be taken, within those limits, in all legal or judicial considerations, as the highest rule of action.

§ 10. Since the whole variety of human interests and action cannot, from their nature, be distinctly divided among and included under the limits of different states,[1] the powers of society, in reference to such interests and action as are beyond the separate control of single states, can only be exercised among states recognizing no superior among themselves, by a united, or reciprocal reference to principles of antecedent authority and universal obligation. They must, therefore, refer to the conditions of man's existence (a law in the secondary sense), and to human reasoning in regard to those conditions, as giving the only law (independent of agreements which themselves rest on that law for their obligation) which can be recognized as a rule of action and one of natural origin—an origin distinct from their own juridical will. But because they recognize no superior among themselves in determining that law of nature, the only exposition of it which can have *legal* force—that is, a force like

---

city, or at most, of a province. For a justification of this use of the term *national law*, compare Bentham's Morals and Legislation, ch. xviii., 26. Reddie's Inquiries &c., pp. 93, 94, 236, and the same author's Historical View of the Law of Marit. Commerce, p. 1.

With jurists who have used the Latin language, *jus civile* is employed as the equivalent of that which is here denominated *national* law, as by Grotius, B. et P. Proleg., § 1 : "Jus civile, sive Romanum, sive quod cuique patrium est" &c., and compare Hobbes' definition of *jus civile* (ante § 7, n.) The term has generally the same force with the classical Roman jurists : but it was also sometimes used by them in other senses, as will be shown hereafter, (ch. iv.,) and compare Smith's Dict. Antiq., Jus. The name "civil law" cannot well be given to that which is here called *national* law, since it is already used to indicate the Roman law, or the Roman law as generally received in Europe, in contradistinction with English common law, and is also employed to designate that portion of the law which does not include punitive, or the so-called "criminal" law.

[1] Bowyer: Univ. Pub. Law, p. 139: "For it is impossible to confine the effects of municipal laws absolutely within the territories of each state; and, therefore, the laws of different countries have points of contact which arise from the general intercourse of mankind, and may be looked upon as a necessary part of the scheme of laws which regulate the world, divided as it is into independent nations and sovereignties."

that of *the law*, in the ordinary sense, as above defined—must be that which has been allowed by such states; each constituting an independent authority in ascertaining the true principles of that law.[1]

From this mutual acknowledgment of principles of natural law, and the agreement of sovereign states founded on them, arises that which is properly called *international* law, in respect to its objects and jurisdiction, but oftener, perhaps, the "law of nations:" a name usually taken to be more appropriate because the term may mean either a law of which nations are the authors, or one of which nations are the subjects. And, indeed, this law limits in some respects, and in others extends, the action or authority of separate nations and sovereignties; but while it derives its force and origin mainly from principles necessarily acknowledged among nations as having the character of a pre-existent natural law, it still is made to have the effect or actual force of law by the action of those nations, since each claims an equal right to define or interpret the supposed natural law, equivalent to equal power of legislation.[2]

§ 11. When this international law or law of nations is viewed as a rule of conduct between nations or states as the subjects of

---

[1] 7 Cranch, 136–7. Marshall, J. Bentham (Morals and Legisl., c. 19, § 2) proposed to use international law in this sense, following D'Aguesseau, (Œuv., T. i., p. 445,) writing, 1757. and Dr. Zouch, 1650, who distinguished *jus inter gentes* from *jus gentium;* see Reddie: Elem. International Law; Wheaton's I. L.; Wildman's Institutes of do.; Fœlix, Droit International Privé, § 1.

Bl. Com., B. I.: Intro., p. 43, B. iv., 67. Suarez: De Legibus, etc., Lib. ii., c. 2, 9. "Nunquam enim civitates sunt sibi tam sufficientes quam indigeant mutuo juvamine et societate, interdum ad majorem utilitatem, interdum ob necessitatem moralem. Hac igitur ratione indigent aliquo jure quo dirigantur et recte ordinentur in hoc genere societatis. Et quamvis magna ex parte hoc fiat per rationem naturalem non tamen sufficienter et immediate quoad omnia, ideoque specialia jura poterant usu earundem gentium introduci." Whewell: El. of Moral. &c., B. II., ch. vi., § 214. "But the general rules and analogies of natural *Jus* lead to determinations of the rights and obligations of nations which form a body of acknowledged law. This body of law is *Jus inter gentes*, and may be termed—International *Jus*."

[2] Pufendorf: Droit de la Nat. et des Gens., l. 2, c. iii., § 7. Grotius: B. et P. Proleg., § 17. "Et hoc jus est quod gentium dicitur, quoties id nomen a jure naturali distinguimus." Grotius here refers to *international* law, the law of which nations are the subjects, and arises from their consent—"ita inter civitates, aut omnes aut plerasque, ex consensu jura quædam nasci potuerunt"—in the same section, defining this *jus gentium*. In other places, Grotius speaks of the term *jus gentium* as being used for what he calls *jus naturale*, as ch. i., § 14—"jus naturale, quod ipsum quoque gentium dici solet;" in same chapter, § 11, 1, he notices the distinction made in the Roman law between *jus naturale* and *jus gentium*, considering it as out of use, "usum vix ullum habet." The necessity of preserving each of these significations of *jus gentium* will be shown hereinafter in this chapter and in the second.

that law, and is compared with the municipal law of any one of those states in reference to the relation of superior and inferior, which is a pre-existent condition of law in the sense of a rule of action: or, in other words, when its *authority* is compared with that of the municipal (national) law of any one state as the rule of action within its own dominion or national limits, it is at once seen that the international law, in this point of view, is not strictly *a law;* since the mutual independence of nations precludes the idea of that relative superiority and inferiority.[1] It is only a rule of moral obligation for nations or states in their political existence.[2] But so far as this international law affects the actions of individuals, and is enforced by the authority of some state, it becomes a law in the strict sense, and at the same time becomes identified with municipal law, in becoming a part of the law enforced by a state within its own domain or national jurisdiction.

§ 12. It is only, therefore, as a law *between* states, as its subjects, that international law has a separate existence from municipal law: and in this application of the international law it receives the name of a law only by way of analogy: that is, it is only analogous to a law in the proper sense. When international law is enforced by some state within its own national limits, as a law in the strict sense, it is then distinguished from the municipal law only by its having a different application and effect. Its legal authority, whenever it acts as a law in the proper sense, is identified with that of some municipal (national) law, or the law prevailing, territorially, under the exclusive dominion of some nation.[3]

§ 13. The distinction thus made in the law, of being international and municipal, indicates, at the same time, the various nature of its jurisdiction, or the variety in the objects and interests which it affects, and the difference in the nature of its origin, as either in the associated or separate authority of nations or states. And, though this distinction is not founded upon a

---

[1] Rayneval: Instit. du droit de la nature et des gens, note 10, du 1 Liv., p. viii. Wheaton: Internat. Law, p. 17. D'Aguesseau: Œuvres, Tom. I., p. 445.

[2] Reddie: Histor. View L. of Marit. Com., p. 24. Hence called by Austin: Prov. Jurisp., p. 207, a law of "positive morality."

[3] Reddie's Inquiries in International Law, 2d ed., p. 412, 466.

LAW OF NATURE RECOGNIZED. 11

difference in the origin of the law, as being in part derived from natural principles, or principles of ethics, and in part from the will of society, neither does it imply a denial of the moral foundation of either of these divisions of the law in the obligation of natural rules of action. On the contrary, each of these manifestations of the power of society rather asserts their existence and authority: justifying that power on the ground that those rules are made efficacious by such manifestation.[1]

The international law, otherwise called "the law of nations," in the sense of a rule of which states are the subjects, as well as the municipal law of any one state, may or may not be consistent with the true dictates of natural reason, or what ought to be received among all nations as natural law. Each of these divisions of the law has changed, while constantly claiming to agree with those principles. Whatever may have been the speculative opinions of philosophers, natural law, or right, has always been confessed by states and jurists to exist, and to be of constant obligation;[2] but has had effect as *law*, in the sense of the subject and guide of judicial decision, only so far as acknowledged by sovereign powers, nations, or states.

§ 14. It is not here denied that the true law of nature, the unchangeable dictates of just reason, being, by the supposition, co-existent with the nature of man, must be constantly binding on all mankind, independently of the provisions of human law.[3] The nature of the mind being such that man is capable of moral choice independently of all earthly power.[4] The agreement of the human law with the natural or divine precepts must in each case be a question which each person, subject to both, must determine in his own conscience for himself; though the human law may not allow his decision to have any practical effect in

---

[1] Compare, on this question, Phillimore: Internat. Law, Introduction, and ch. iii.

[2] Lieber: Pol. Eth., B. i, § 39, 40, 41. Bowyer: Univ. Public Law, ch. iv. Reddie's Inquiries Elem. &c., p. 9, 58.

[3] Austin: Prov. of Jurisp., p. 280, n. 4. "All the older writers on the so-called law of nations incessantly blend and confound international law as it *is*, with international law as it *ought* to be; with that indeterminate something which they suppose it *would* be, if it conformed to that indeterminate something which they style the law of nature."

Von Martens was the first writer who pointed out the necessity of avoiding this confusion. See Martens: Law of Nations, ch. i. Reddie: Inq. in International Law, ch. ii.; and Austin, continuation of note cited.

[4] Lieber's Pol. Eth., B. iv., c. 2.

excusing a violation of its own provisions; it being essential to its own existence that it should itself decide as to such agreement, and enforce its own commands without regard to any other judgment. And in this respect it is immaterial whether the individual opposes to the will of the state his single judgment of the natural law, or refers to a recognized body, or church, as authoritative in such questions. The authority of such church in matters of *law*, resting on its being supported by, or identified with, the supreme power of the state; and in the absence of such identification, acting on the individual by his voluntary choice, or the judgment of his conscience.[1]

§ 15. Municipal law, according to Blackstone's definition, is "a rule of civil conduct prescribed by the supreme power in a state, commanding what is right, and prohibiting what is wrong." The latter clause of this definition has been criticised as superfluous, if that be right which the supreme power may call such; or inconsistent, in denying the supremacy of that called supreme, by implying another legal criterion of right than its own judgment. And in Blackstone's analysis of this definition, speaking of "the declaratory part"—"declaring what is right, and prohibiting what is wrong," he says, "it depends not so much upon the law of revelation or of nature as on the will of the legislature."

The supreme power in the state must necessarily be absolute, in being subject to no judge.[2] It may give to its own will the name of right, and enforce it as law; but as the essential conditions of man's nature, and the ends of society, must always be the same,—to support which states exist, a violation or denial of their existence would be to the same degree a destruction of the basis of the state, and would free the individual subject from the obligation of obedience. The limits of the definition are a question of political ethics rather than any part of a view of the *law;* which should be a statement of *what is*, rather than

---

[1] D'Aguesseau: Œuv., Tom. i., p. 688. There are, of course, many writers who might be cited against this view. Compare Bowyer's Univ. Pub. Law, p. 73—87. Bunsen's Signs of the Times, ch. v.
[2] Lessee of Livingston *v.* Moore and others, 7 Peters R., 546. Johnson J.—" The power existing in every body politic is an absolute despotism." Paley: Mor. and Pol. Phil., B. vi., c. 6. Bodin: Repub., B. i., c. 8. Austin: Prov. Jur., p. 295.

of *what ought to be ;*[1] for which purpose the abridged definition is comprehensive enough—"municipal law is a rule of action prescribed by the highest power of a state;"[2] not regarding it as capable of being wrong: that is, not judging it by any rule out of itself.[3]

The supreme power of a state, or, more correctly, the person or persons holding that power, may always claim to interpret their own legislation by a reference to natural law, as having been always the guide and exponent of their intention. And in every sovereign nationality this power must exist, and be somewhere vested. Such interpretation from the source of the law is practically identified with the sovereign act of legislation. But the administrators of the law, as subordinates of this sovereign power, or of its possessors, either executive or judicial, cannot assume to themselves the right of annulling, by a decision under the law of nature appealing to their consciences, the decrees of that sovereignty which gives them their powers, and determines the limits of their judgment.[4] And where, by the law of that sovereign will, the ordinary course of legislation is delegated to limited governments, the possessors of legislative power cannot alter the limits assigned to them on grounds derived from the law of nature.[5] So far, however, as the supreme power adopts the natural law in the expression of its own will, and, which is essential to such adoption, refers to a settled interpretation of it, it becomes municipal, or international law, and the rule for private action and judicial decision.[6]

---

[1] Quid sit juris, non quid sit justum aut injustum. Austin: Prov. Jur., p. 276.

[2] Kent's Comm., Lect. xx., *pr.* "Municipal law is a rule of civil conduct prescribed by the supreme power of a state."

[3] Co. Lit., fo. 110, a: Of the power of Parliament, "Que il est de tres grand honor et justice, et que nul doit imaginer chose dishonorable:" cites Pl. Com., 398, b. Doctor and Student, ca. 55, fol. 164. Compare a summary of various authorities on this point in Comment. on Const. and Stat. Law, by E. F. Smith, ch. vii.

[4] Bacon's Essays, 57. Calder *v.* Bull, 3 Dallas, 398. Kant's W., vol. i., Essay on the Faculties.

[5] Fortescue: de Laudibus, ch. xiii.

[6] Austin: Prov. of Jurisprudence Determined, p. 173. "The portion of the positive law, which is parcel of the *law of nature* (or, in the language of the classical jurists, which is parcel of the *jus gentium*) is often supposed to emanate, even as positive law, from a divine, or natural source. But (admitting the distinction of positive law into law natural and law positive) it is manifest that law natural, considered as a portion of positive, is the creature of human sovereigns, and not of the Divine monarch."

§ 17. If natural law were to be recognized in jurisprudence as a rule existing anterior to the will, and independent of the action of states, or society, the portion of law which is confessed to originate solely in the will, or decree of states, might properly be distinguished in jurisprudence as a separate division of *law*.[1] When this distinction is made, such portion is known as *positive* law; which designation is proper for the purpose when the term is understood to refer only to the *origin* of that portion in the will of the state.[2] But if the term *positive* is used to express the authoritative nature of the law, no one part of the law is more entitled to the term than another; it is all equally authoritative, whether a rule of natural origin, or originating in the autonomous decree of the state. If the term is used to mean that which is determined upon by the state as its will,—set, settled upon, *positus*,—positive law includes all law recognized as a judicial rule, or *the law* in the sense herein before given as the ordinary sense, viz., those rules of action which are enforced by the authority of the state.[3] Some term is necessary to express a rule originating in the decree of the state, and since this term *positive law* is commonly used to distinguish such law from rules of natural origin enforced by the state, and is also used to express the whole of law in the ordinary sense, the term *positive law* has become a somewhat ambiguous one. *Positive law* is now used by the best authors to signify every rule that is *law*. Jurisprudence is defined by Austin as being the science of positive law; that is, the science of what the rule given or

---

To say that it emanates as positive law from a Divine, or natural source, is to confound positive law with law whereon it is fashioned, or with law whereunto it conforms."

[1] Grotius: B. et P., Lib. i., c. i., ix. "1. Est et tertia juris significatio quæ idem valet quod lex, quoties vox legis largissime sumitur, ut sit regula actuum moralium obligans ad id quod rectum est," etc. "2. Juris ita accepti optima partitio est quæ apud Aristotelem exstat, ut sit aliud jus naturale, aliud voluntarium, quod ille legitimum vocat, legis vocabulo strictius posito: interdum et τὸ ἐν τάξει, constitutum. Idem discrimen apud Hebræos reperire est," etc.

Hugo: Encyclopædia, p. 16, no. 2, takes jus constitutum, or quod ipse populus sibi constituit, for the Latin term corresponding to what is in the text called *positive law*.

Suarez: De Legibus etc., Lib. i., c. 3, sec. 13.

[2] Compare Neal *v.* Farmer, 9 Georgia R., 575.

D'Aguesseau: Œuvres, Tom. i., p. 260. "Au milieu d'un grand nombre de loix positives fournies par les mœurs des Peuples, ou par la volonté Souveraine du Legislateur." But in the same vol., p. 447, *natural* is discriminated from *positive* law.

[3] 1 Vaughan R., 191, (anno 19 Car. II.) "For the freehold is not a natural thing, but hath its essence by the positive municipal law of the kingdom."

allowed by the state *is*.¹ The science of what *ought to be* the rule is the science of political ethics.²

§ 18. If jurisprudence is taken to be the science of law in the strict and proper sense only (which involves the relation of a superior and inferior, § 1), it is the science of the law of a single nation only, *i. e.*, the science of some one *municipal*, or, more correctly, of some one *national* law;³ and the *international* law is known in jurisprudence only as a subordinate part of some one such national law; or, in other words, the international law is known in jurisprudence only as it may be applied by one national source of law to relations of private persons which grow out of the existence of other nations; since international law is not law in the strict sense, except as it may be enforced by some one nation (ante, § 12). The term *general*, or *universal jurisprudence*, would signify only the aggregated science of different systems of national or municipal law.

§ 19. But since the jurisprudence of each state (as a consequence of its jural character) recognizes natural reason as a rule of intrinsic force,⁴ and in its municipal and international law

---

¹ Savigny: Heut. Rom. Recht, § 5. Austin: Prov. Jurisp., p. 131, and notes; also, p. 197, and *ante*, p. 11, n. 3. Mackeldey, by Kaufmann: Introd., §§ 3, 9, and the notes, distinguishing the philosophy of positive law from philosophical law. Compare Doctor and Student, ch. iv.
Jurisprudence is sometimes used in the sense of the science of abstract right. Long's Discourses, (Law Lib., N. S., vol. 44,) p. 5. "Jurisprudence is the science of right."— Brande's Dict. Mr. Cushing (Introd. to the Study of the Roman Law, Boston, 1854, p. 6) takes it in the sense of the application of law to particular cases; and, in p. 168, gives it the sense of unwritten law, common law, and judicial law: he also uses the term "jurisprudential" as synonymous with *jural*. With the French lawyers, *jurisprudence* is contrasted with the *lois*, Projet (of the Code Civil), Discours preliminaire, p. xix. * * "On ne peut pas plus se passer de jurisprudence que de lois." Fœlix, Dr.: Int. Pr., p. 382. "Lois positives et jurisprudence." Mr. Reddie uses it in the sense of the whole national law of some state, or the whole of that rule of action which is applied within a certain national domain. Reddie: Inq. El. &c., ch. v. Law Review, London, Nov., 1855, p. 128: "Some term is necessary to denote the science of law, and we shall so employ the word jurisprudence." * * * "By law is here understood positive law,—that is, the law existing by position, or the law of human enactment. Jurisprudence is the science of positive law," &c., citing Suarez: de Leg. etc., L. i., ch. 103, sec. 13.
² "For the wisdom of the law-maker is one, and of a lawyer is another." Bacon: Adv. Learn., Works, Am. Ed., 1 v., 238.
³ Falck: Jurist. Ency., § 11, (French tr.) "Comme le droit prend naissance dans la volonté collective d'une societé civile, il doit y avoir autant de droits qu'il existe de sociétés civiles ou d'etats."
⁴ Bowyer: Univ. Pub. Law, pp. 34, 35. Whewell's Elements Mor. &c., B. ii., ch. vi., § 213. "Since in all nations the definitions of rights and obligations are intended to be right and just, it is natural that there should be much that is common

applies that reason to the unalterable conditions of human existence, thus recognizing the law of nature, in the primary and secondary senses of the word law, it may be anticipated that some principles or rules will be found to be the same in the law of many different states: and these rules, so found to obtain generally, may be distinguished from the rest of the law of any one state by their extent; that is, by their being generally recognized and enforced by the several possessors of the power of society. And though the whole law of each nation is judicially taken to be conformable to natural reason,[1] those principles, when thus known by their general extent, may be judicially considered founded on the necessary conditions of human existence, and therefore be judicially taken as having universal application in all countries, and under the sovereign authority of every nation.[2] They may be considered, in the jurisprudence of any one country, as natural principles; not only because recognized by the national law, but because founded on the general reasoning of men living in the social state.[3] They may, therefore, be considered the subject of a jurisprudence distinct from that of any one nation—a general, or universal jurisprudence; general, or universal, because historically known to prevail among all nations, or among the more powerful and enlightened.[4]

in the views and determination of all nations on the subject. That which is common in the determination of all nations respecting rights and obligations is called *Jus Naturæ*, or *Jus Gentium*. That which is peculiar to the law of a particular state, or city, is called *Jus Civile*, or *Jus Municipale*. We may distinguish these two kinds of Jus as *Natural Jus* and *National Jus*." Also, the same, B. vi., c. i., § 1139.
    [1] Ayliffe's Pandects, p. 6.
    [2] De Tocqueville: Dem. in Am., vol. ii., p. 84. "A general law—which bears the name of Justice—has been made and sanctioned, not only by a majority of this or that people, but by a majority of mankind. * * * A nation may be considered in the light of a jury which is empowered to represent society at large, and to apply the great and general law of Justice."
    In Bowyer's Univ. Pub. Law, ch. iv., where jurisprudence is exhibited by the *a priori* method, following Domat, *universal* jurisprudence is equivalent to political ethics. Duponceau on Jurisdiction, pp. 126, 128, recommending the study of "general jurisprudence," which, he says, is part of the common law, and which he laments "has fallen too much into neglect," does not distinguish it from "universal justice"—"the eternal principles of right and wrong."
    [3] Aristot.: Rhet., L. i., c. 13. 15. Reddie's Inq. Elem., &c., 85-87.
    [4] Here universal jurisprudence is derived by reasoning *a posteriori*, according to Grotius' method; and, so derived, it has no necessary identity with that derived *a priori*, in the manner pursued by Domat, (see Loix civiles; Tr. des Loix, and the summary given by Bowyer, Univ. Pub. Law, p. 68,) and also by Pufendorf, and others,

§ 20. The term *law of nations, jus gentium*, had been originally employed by the Roman jurists to designate legal principles having this general extent, before it became applied to that

as Manning: *v.* Comm. Writers on international law, or the law of nations, in the same sense, may be divided into two classes: those who derive it *a priori* are, however, properly speaking, writers on *ethics*; those only who derive it *a posteriori* are writers on *law*. Law determined in the manner pursued by the last is derived by the inductive method, or empirically, in the language of the German writers. (For a similar distinction among writers on political and religious systems, compare La Mennais: Essai sur l'Indifference &c., Tom. ii., p. 158. De Maistre: Soirees de St. Petersburg, Tom. i., p. 280.)

Bowyer's Comm. on Mod. Civil Law, Lond., 1848, p. 26. "The Romans give the reason of the universality of what they call the law of nations in these words,—quod naturalis ratio inter omnes homines constituit. But the civilians of modern times have drawn their classification from the reason of the alleged universality of the law, and not from that universality itself, which, owing to the ignorance of some nations, does not in point of fact exist. That reason is, because the obligatory force of the law is pointed out by the mental faculties of man. This universally obligatory law (though not universally observed) is called *natural law*, and is thus defined by Grotius," &c., citing B. et P., Lib. i., c. i., § 10. i. Now Grotius clearly distinguishes in § 12, of the same chapter, between these *two methods of ascertaining* the law; and though he is the leading author following the inductive method, he still attributes *its authority*, when ascertained, to nature, or to the Creator, not to the will of political states. The question, what rules do the mental faculties of man declare to be obligatory? is solved by the history of man's exercise of his mental faculties, and not by the mental faculties of the individual jurist. Mr. Reddie adheres to what may be called the early Roman school, and insists that the modern civilians have erred so far as they have derived their jus gentium *a priori*. Showing, too, that, in fact, the principles of the law of nature, as unfolded by Pufendorf, Cocceius, Wolf, and others, are little else than propositions taken from the Roman law; stripped of all that identified them with the national system of the Romans. (Reddie's Inq. Elem. &c., 74–76, 81.) Gravina declares, De Ortu &c., L. i., Princip.: "Quoniam nihil aliud est jus civile, nisi naturalis ad Romanæ Reipublicæ institutionem relata, Romanisque moribus et literis explicata ratio," etc.

Bentham: Moral and Leg., ch. xvii. "Of what stamp are the works of Grotius, Pufendorf, and Burlamaqui? Are they political or ethical, historical or judicial, expository or censorial? Sometimes one thing, sometimes another; they seem hardly to have settled the matter with themselves. A defect this, to which all books must almost unavoidably be liable which take for their subject the pretended *law of nature*; an obscure phantom, which, in the imaginations of those who go in chase of it, points sometimes to *manners*, sometimes to *laws*; sometimes to what law *is*, sometimes to what it *ought to be*." And the author here refers to ch. ii., 14, of the same work, and his note to the passage, which is herein before cited, p. 6; and compare Morhof's Polyhistor, vol. iii., Lib. vi, c. 1. De Jurisprudentiæ universalis Scriptoribus.

Grotius is not, indeed, altogether constant to the method indicated in the passage referred to. Grotius: B. et P., ch. i., 12. "Now that any thing is, or is not the law of nature, is generally proved either *a priori*,—that is, by argument drawn from the very nature of the thing; or *a posteriori*,—that is, by reasons taken from something external. The former way of reasoning is more subtile and abstracted; the latter, more popular. The proof by the former is by showing the necessary fitness or unfitness of any thing with a reasonable and sociable nature. But the proof by the latter is, when we cannot with absolute certainty, yet with very great probability, conclude that to be the law of nature which is generally believed to be so by all, or, at least, the most civilized nations. For a universal effect requires a universal cause; and there cannot well be any other cause assigned for this general opinion than what is called common sense."

law which is herein before called the international law, and which had not with the Romans any recognized existence, as distinct from their own public law, *jus publicum Romanum.* These principles will always constitute a part of the international law, the rules of which are in a great degree founded on their existence, as will be shown in the next chapter. But they exist independently of it, and are equally a constituent part of municipal (national) law.[1] There will always be a necessity for their distinct recognition, and for some appropriate term by which to distinguish them. The term *universal law* has been employed by late English writers to designate these principles, corresponding to the *law of nations, jus gentium,* of the Roman jurists.[2]

§ 21. Law, in being a rule of action, necessarily regards both agents and objects of action; and thus in its inception constitutes the first distinction known to the law, in determining who or what are agents, and who or what are the objects of

---

[1] D'Aguesseau: Œuvres, Tom. i., p. 444. Duponceau on Jurisdiction, pp. 18, 110, 126, 128. Compare, also, Bacon: De Augmentis, Lib. viii., De justitia universali, seu de fontibus juris. Selden: De J. nat. et Gen. &c., Lib. i., c. iii., vi.

[2] Bentham uses the term *universal* to describe those principles which are commonly received among all nations. See Morals and Legislat., ch. xviii., 24. " In the first place, in point of extent, what is delivered concerning the laws in question may have reference either to the laws of such or such a nation, or nations, in particular, or to the laws of all nations whatsoever; in the first case, the book may be said to relate to *local*, in the other to universal jurisprudence."

"Ealra theoda riht, (the right of all nations,) *jus gentium.*" Bosworth's Lexicon Anglo-Sax., verb, *Riht.*

There is no classic Greek term answering to the Latin *jus.* νόμος corresponds to *lex*. The distinction between a jus ἴδιον, proprium, id est populis vel civitatibus singulis civile, and a jus κοινὸν, commune, is remarked by Aristotle, Rhet., Lib. i., c. 13, 15, where he also designates the latter as being that which is κατὰ φύσιν, secundum naturam; but recognizing it to be so from the fact that it is universally received. Comp. Thuc., B. iii., 59, τὰ κοινὰ τῶν Ἑλλήνων νόμιμα. The Byzantine jurists, who, about A. D. 876, prepared the Greek version of the Corpus Juris, known as the Basilica, (v. Smith: Dict. Antiq. Butler's Horæ Juridica, app. iv.,) used the term νόμιμον ἐθνικὸν, and also coined from juris-gentium the word Ἰουρισγεντίος. See Selden: De J. Nat. et Gent. &c., Lib. i., c. vi.

Brougham: Polit. Philos., Prelim. Disc. "It is a very common error to confound with this branch of the law" [referring to *international law*, here denominated by Lord Brougham "the law of nations,"] many of those general principles of jurisprudence common to all nations, and to term these a portion of the law of nations." With equal justice it may be said the error lies in calling *international law* by the name "law of nations;" or rather, it lies in calling by one name two distinct sets of legal principles, viz., principles known, or denominated from their general recognition, or application by nations, and those rules which are applied as a law between nations; which last are derived both from the first—the principles universally recognized—and from the agreements and customs of particular states.

action. Agents, under a rule of action for moral beings, being necessarily such as are considered by the author of the rule capable of choice and action; or *persons*, to be distinguished from *things:* the latter being only the objects of action, and incapable of personality—that is, of capacity for choice and action.

The action of persons may be in direct relation to other persons as the objects of action; and even in relation to things, as such objects, is of legal significance only in respect to other persons. In other words, all legal relations are relations of persons to persons—directly, or through things.[1]

§ 22. A legal relation between persons consists in a privilege and obligation as mutually essential. This privilege and obligation exist in each of these classes of relations, constituting rights and duties as correlative, or as necessary co-efficients of each other.[2]

When rights and duties are classified, they must always be taken as rights and duties of persons, since it is only by the prior recognition of persons that relations, privileges, and obligation can be said to exist. Rights and duties cannot be separately classified in any system of jurisprudence, because, being correlative, they cannot be separately described; the definition of one is involved in the definition of the other.

§ 23. The prominent distinction between rights (with their correlative duties) is that of being rights in relations wherein persons are the objects of action, and rights in relations wherein things are the objects of action. But since persons and things are associated in every action of natural persons, it is impossible to make an accurate classification on this distinction.[3] Rights

---

[1] Ahrens: Naturrecht, p. 83. *Tr.* "A being endowed with self-consciousness, reason, and freedom [power of choice] is called a person, or has personality."
"The law relates to persons as its groundwork and aim, (Zweck.) That is, it has an essentially personal character. The distinction which is ordinarily made between the law of persons and the law of things, as of two co-ordinate parts of the law, is therefore inaccurate. All law is throughout a law of persons."
"The law necessarily relates to things also, inasmuch as these compose the physical conditions of human development. But the law relative to things constitutes only a subordinate division of the law relating to persons."

[2] Jus et obligatio sunt correlata. Thibaut: Syst. Pand. Rechts, Elementary Part, § 1. (Lindley's Transl. in vol. 86 of Law Library.)

[3] Compare Austin: Prov. of Jurisp., Appendix, xviii.—xxv. Wesenbecii Comm. ad Pandect, Lib. i., tit. v., num. 1, n. "Omne jus quo utimur, vel ad per-

considered without reference to specific things as the objects of action may be called *rights of persons*, and distinguished from rights considered with reference to specific things, or classes of things, as the objects of action: which may in a certain sense be called *rights of things;* meaning, however, rather the relations of things to persons having rights and duties in respect to those things.[1]

§ 24. A right may be considered as to its subject or its object. The subject of a right is the person in relation to whom it exists; its object is the matter to which it relates.[2]

Persons, both as agents and objects of action, are the subjects of rights. Things can only be the objects of rights, as well as the objects of action.

As, from the nature of *things*, they can be regarded in a rule of action only so far as they are in the power and possession of agents, or persons, property is an essential attribute of the nature of *things*.[3]

---

sonas pertinet quibus jus redditur, vel ad res de quibus jus redditur, vel ad actiones sive judicia per quæ jus redditur." Here, in the first instance, *jus* signifies the jural rule; afterwards, it has the sense of a right, or privilege.

See Reddie's Inquiries Elem. &c., pp. 146—159, for the distribution or arrangement of private law made by Gaius, Grotius, Bodinus, Bacon, Leibnitz, Coccieus, Pothier, and Millar of Glasgow.

[2] Reddie's Inq. Elem. &c., p. 171. "Now rights and obligations are manifestly the attributes of persons, not of things. And to divide rights, like Judge Blackstone, into the rights of persons and the rights of things, if by the latter words are meant rights, not over, in or to, but belonging to, or inherent, and vested in things, we have seen, either evinces inaccuracy of thought, or is, at best, misapplication of language. Again, rights and obligations are not merely the attributes of persons singly; they pre-suppose and exist only in reference to other persons. A single man existing on the surface of this earth would have certain physical powers over external things, but no legal rights."

"But although rights and obligations are in reality, and correctly, the relations of individual persons, to other individuals, they are plainly correlative terms."

Hale, whom Blackstone followed in this distribution, used also the Latin terms *jura rerum* and *jura personarum*. The word *jus* signifies law, as well as a right—the effect of law. *Jura rerum*, in the sense of the law relating to things, would have a meaning. Compare 1 Starke's Ev., p. 1, n. b. Austin: Prov. of J., append. xix.

[2] In the languages of which the Latin is the principal basis, (the *Romance* languages,) *subject* (e. g. *sujet*, Fr.) is commonly used to designate that which is here called the *object* of a right. Mackeldey's Civil Law, Comp. Introd., § 14. "In connection with every right, we find a subject and an object. The subject of the right is the person on whom the right is conferred; the object of a right is the matter to which it relates." The German writers generally, when employing the words as German words, use them in the manner here followed in the text. See Hugo: Encycl., p. 11. Lindley's Translation of Thibaut, append. ii.

[3] Compare on these sections, Long's Disc., p. 109—115. Coode on Legislative Expression, p. 9.

§ 25. By regarding states, or sovereign powers, as determining either the laws of their own existence, or the rules of action for persons subject to their supremacy, international and municipal (national) law may each be divided into two parts—viz., *public* and *private;* though, since the relations of individual persons are in the end the objects of each division, the distinction cannot throughout be accurately observed.[1] It is, perhaps, more correct to say, municipal (national) and international law may each be distinguished as either public or private law, according to the public or private character of the persons whom it affects.[2]

That may be called *private municipal* (national) law which determines, within the limits of a state, the relations of persons towards each other in all incidents of the social state distinct from the political existence of the supreme power.

The *public* part of *municipal* (national) law is that by which the supreme power defines or asserts its own nature, bounds, and purposes within its own limits; and the investiture or seat of that power; either, as existing undivided, or centralized in a whole people, or in a larger or smaller portion of it, or in a single family, or person; or, as being divided and distributed, according to its objects, among various depositaries.

[1] Mackeldey's Compend. Introd., § 8. "With respect to its object, all positive law may be divided into public and private law. The public law (*jus publicum*) comprehends those rules of law which relate to the constitution and government of the state; consequently, it concerns only the relations of the people to the government. The private law (*jus privatum*) comprehends those rules which pertain to the juridical relations of citizens among themselves." This division of the law into public and private is found in the Institutes, and observed principally in the writings of the civilians. If not very philosophical, or distinctive, it is convenient, especially in treating of conditions of freedom, or its opposites; which are spoken of in a political, as well as a social connection. It is not, however, essential that the subject of jurisprudence should be thus divided. Austin, in Prov. Jurisp., Appendix, lxi., observes: "As I shall show, also, every department of law, viewed from a certain aspect, may be styled private; whilst every department of law, viewed from another aspect, may be styled public. As I shall show further, *public* law and *private law* are names which should be banished the science; for since each will apply indifferently to every department of law, neither can be used conveniently to the purpose of signifying any. As I shall show, moreover, the entire corpus juris ought to be divided at the outset into law of things and law of persons; whilst the only portion of law that can be styled *public law* with a certain, or determinate meaning, ought not to be contradistinguished with the law of things and persons, but ought to be inserted in the law of persons as one of its limbs, or members."

Mr. Reddie: Inquiries Element. &c., 261-2, regards the distinction between public and private law as essential in every system.

[2] Savigny: Heut. Rom. Recht, B. i., c. 2, § 9. The German term bürgerliches Recht corresponds to *private law*. Heffter: Europ. Völkerr., § 37.

The *private international* law[1] determines the relations of individuals towards other national authorities or jurisdictions than that with which by the public municipal and international law they are primarily associated as subjects; and constitutes, in connection with the private municipal law, the rules of ordinary peaceful intercourse of nations as composed of private individuals.

Public international law is that which concerns the mutual relations of sovereign states or powers, as such; determining the nature of such relations, and, for the purpose of maintaining them, furnishing the rules of diplomatic intercourse and military arbitrament.

By these two divisions of *public* law, in various forms of expression, have been determined the territorial limits for the exclusive sovereignty of different nations, in legitimating acts of force, or agreement, as being rightful in their own nature, or in their existing results.

§ 26. The distinction of the law as being municipal (national) and international is founded on the separation of society into states occupying certain distinct geographical limits, or portions of territory: the two branches, municipal (national) and international, each contemplate the agents and objects of action according to the territorial jurisdiction under which they may be found. The international law recognizing states as having authority within certain territory, and persons as primarily subject to one or another system of municipal (national) law according to their locality. In this view laws are *territorial* in their nature, as having effect within certain geographical limits.

But law is always in its nature personal, or a law for certain persons. *Jurisdiction* is a term signifying the authority of law over a certain territory, or over certain persons; but since the action of persons must always be the essential object of all laws, the jurisdiction of laws over a certain territory means over all persons within that territory.

---

[1] The use of the term Private International Law is now very generally received; vide 1 Kent's Comm., p. 2, referring to M. Victor Faucher. See, also, an article by the latter on Private International Law, in Am. Jurist, vol. xx., p. 33. Story: Conf. Laws, p. 9. Phillimore: International Law, Pref. xv., and p. 12. Fœlix: Tr. du Droit International Privé, § 1. "Le droit international se divise en droit public et en droit privé." Schæffner: Entwicklung des Internationalen Privat Rechts; Frankfort, 1841. Heffter: Europ. Völkerr., § 38. Waechter, in Archiv. f. civil. Praxis, Bd. 24, 25.

And though laws are known as rules having a coercive force only in and for some particular geographical district, they may be spoken of, or classified and distinguished, by their application to particular persons. Laws in establishing relations among men, necessarily establish differences between them as the subjects or objects of the rights and obligations composing those relations, and persons under any system of law may be classed according to the differences which it recognizes among them; and the law itself may be distinguished as attaching to certain persons, or as being divided into different *personal* laws, as well as being the territorial law of some national jurisdiction.

§ 27. This distinction of laws as personal may obtain both in national (municipal) and international law; and it is essential when those divisions are contrasted with each other as the constituent parts of private law—i. e., law applying to private persons. The national (municipal) law, which, according to the definition of it before given, applies to persons as the law of a certain territory, may create a variety of relations for different individuals; and when the international law (which is law in an imperfect sense only when states are regarded as its subjects) is applied or enforced by some state within its own territory, and becomes a law acting on private persons, it is necessarily applied as a personal law; because it is applied by recognizing persons as connected with different nations, and by way of exception to the territorial, or municipal law of some one state. So far as it exists distinct, within any one jurisdiction, from the national law thereof,—it applies as a personal law.

So far as any legal principles which are included in the universal law, or "*law of nations,*" establish relations for, or between particular persons, they also may be considered as a

[1] Hobbes: Leviath. De Civitate, c. xxvi. "Legum autem alia civibus statuitur universis; alia certis provinciis; alia certo hominum generi; alia homini quandoque singulari." Story: Conflict of Laws, § 51. Bowyer's Univ. Public L., p. 144–7. Hamilton's Hedaya: Introductory Disc., respecting personal laws in Hindostan; and Stat. 21, Geo. III., ch. 70, relating to Inhabitants of British India. Sir Wm. Jones: Inst. of Hindu Law, art. 203. Savigny: Geschichte d. R. R. im Mittelalter, Bd. i., p. 115. Canciani: Leges Barbarorum Antiq., vol. i., p. 345. Sachsenspiegel—Schwabenspiegel: Ancient Collections of the customary law of the Saxons and Suabians. The jurisprudence of the Middle Ages was characterized by the personal extent of laws; and, as matter of history, the personal extent of law has been anterior to its territorial extent. See Savigny: Heut. Rom. R., § 346.

personal law, taking effect by their recognition by separate states, or nations, each applying them in municipal, or international law, as before defined.

§ 28. Although it is herein before assumed that natural law has no recognition in jurisprudence as *legally authoritative,* except as it is supported by the power of society, or of the state, and therefore, when legally or judicially operative, must be identified with positive law, yet it is also considered as being true in point of fact that all sovereign states have acknowledged in some form the pre-existence of natural principles of right, and as the originators of positive law have claimed to correspond with them. Among authors and legislators these principles have always been recognized under names indicating the difference of their *origin* from that strictly called positive law, such as the law of nature, the divine law, the law of right reason, &c.[1]

Whether all interpretation of these principles, given by sovereign states in their municipal laws, can be considered as actually corresponding with the real divine, or natural rule, which they suppose to be pre-existing, may be judged from the various decisions which successive generations of lawgivers have passed on the acts of their predecessors, each in turn founding their own judgments and corrections upon a claim to more just views of truth and right reason.

§ 29. The application of jurisprudence to the relations of persons and things is in most modern states made by judicial tribunals, distinct from the supreme legislating authority of the state.[2] But whatever rules or principles such tribunals may apply as law, they apply them as being the will of the supreme authority, and as being themselves only the instruments of that will. The will of the state is to be ascertained by the tribunal in one of the following methods:—

First. Direct, or positive legislation, is the first and ruling indication of the will of the state, whether it acknowledges or refers to any rule of natural origin or not.

Second. Since the will of the state is to be presumed to

---

[1] Grotius: B. et P., Lib. i., c. i., § 10. D'Aguesseau: Œuv., Tom. i., pp. 446—449, Premiere Instruc. Whewell: Pol. and Mor., § 477. Cicero: De Rep., iii., 22.
[2] Lieber: Political Ethics, § 133. Pascal: Lettres Provinciales, xiv.

accord with natural law, where the positive legislation of the state does not decide, the tribunal must ascertain the natural law which is to be enforced as the will of the state.[1] But this law can only be determined by such *criteria* as are supposed to be recognized by the supreme power of the state, if such criteria exist; and this law when so determined becomes identified in its *authority* with positive law.[2]

If a state is supposed to be in the commencement of its existence as a state administering law, or governing by law, the only exposition of this natural law would be the reason and conscience of the judicial tribunal.[3]

§ 30. But since every judgment of the tribunal which has been executed and upheld by the power of the state must be received as accordant with its will, every such judgment becomes an indication of the natural law, as received by the state, and, therefore, equal in authority, for the judgment of future tribunals, to the law received by positive legislation. Tribunals established by the state have, therefore, of necessity, a *quasi*-legislative power; or—the tribunal, the object of whose institution is to apply the law given by the state, is incidentally a source of law.[4]

But there is this difference between its powers in this respect and those of the state itself, that the latter is not, in any *legal*

---

[1] To use the terms of Roman jurisprudence—the law proceeding from the legislator is expressed by *esto;* that proceeding from the tribunal by *videtur.* Bacon de Aug. Sc., Lib. viii., c. 3, 10. Aphorismus 32. "Curiæ sunto et jurisdictiones quæ statuant, ex arbitrio boni viri et discretione sana, ubi legis norma deficit. Lex enim, ut antea dictum est, non sufficit casibus sed ad ea quæ plerumque accidunt aptatur. Sapientissima autem res Tempus, (ut ab antiquis dictum est,) et novorum casuum quotidie auctor et inventor."

[2] Ram on Judgment, p. 2 : "A judgment that is constructed of certain materials which are law, and is, when delivered, a part of the law of the land." Legislation is first in respect to authority, but in the natural order of existence the judicial rule appears first. Reddie's Inquiries, &c., p. 110—112.

[3] See Encyc. Am., vol. vii., pp. 576, 580, 586. Appendix; Law, Legislation, Codes: by Judge Story—do. p. 584. "The legislation of no country probably ever gave origin to its whole body of laws. In the formation of society, the principles of natural justice and the obligations of good faith must have been recognized before any common legislature was acknowledged," &c. Cushing : Introd. to Study of the Roman Law. Boston, 1854, p. 22.

[4] Reddie's Inq. Elem. &c., p. 193–5. Bentham, objecting against this source of law, calls the common law, a law *ex post facto :* see Papers relative to Codification, No. I., § 3, and Reddie's Inq. Elem. &c., Suppl., p. 104. Dig. L. i., Tit. 4, § 38. Consuetudinem, aut rerum perpetuo similiter judicatarum auctoritatem, vim legis obtinere debere.

sense, *bound* by any previous interpretation of the natural law, and is, in the theory of jurisprudence, to be considered as the criterion of the provisions of that law, while the tribunal is presumed always to follow standards of interpretation of natural law already acknowledged or accepted by the state, so far as they exist.[1]

The decision made by any judicial tribunal may, therefore, be always compared by succeeding tribunals with other standards of natural law which are presumed, equally with that decision, to indicate the natural law as received by the state. With the lapse of time, by the accumulation of concurrent expositions of the natural law, the power of each tribunal, successively to make law in this incidental manner, becomes more limited; because the recognition of natural law by the state, through anterior tribunals, has become more definite by being more widely applied.[2]

§ 31. The principle by which judicial precedent becomes an exposition of the legal rule of action, is also that which causes *custom* to be juridically recognized as having the coercive force of positive law. It is not that any number of similar actions

---

[1] Bentham: Morals and Legislation, ch. xvii., 20 (of Appendix to the original ed., 1823, vol. ii., p. 274). "In that enormous mass of confusion and inconsistency, the ancient Roman, or, as it is termed, by way of eminence, *the civil* law, the imperative matter and even all traces of the imperative character, seem at last to have been smothered in the expository. *Esto* had been the language of primæval simplicity: *esto* had been the language of the twelve tables. By the time of Justinian (so thick was the darkness raised by a cloud of commentators), the penal law had been crammed into an odd corner of the civil—the whole catalogue of offences, and even of crimes, lay buried under a heap of *obligations—will* was hid in *opinion*—and the original *esto* had transformed itself into *videtur* in the mouths of even the most despotic sovereigns." It depends upon the intention, whether this was blamable or not. It was perhaps only an affectation on the part of the prince to speak like an expounder of existing law when called upon, by an exercise of autonomic juridical power, to relieve the law of obscurity, caused by conflicting opinions of juridical persons who were not sovereign.

[2] Ram: Legal Judg., c. i., xiv. Bacon, de Aug. Lib., viii., c. 8, 10. Aphor., 21—31. Lindley's Thibaut, Append., xii., and note. Falck: Jurist. Ency., § 10. (French Tr.): "A côté du droit coutumier vient se placer la *practique judiciaire*, *Gerichts-gebrauch*, l'usage du palais, (*usus fori*, *Observanz*, *stylus curiæ*) c'est à dire, l'ensemble des règles de droit qui se forment par la practique uniforme des functionaires publics dans les affaires juridiques.

"Les maximes ainsi établies ont aussi force des lois; mais quand commencent elles à l'avoir ? C'est ce qu'il n'est pas possible de préciser ; tout se reduit à ceci; il faut que le nombre des *précédents* (præjudicatæ) soit suffisant pour constituer une opinion sur un point de droit. Il est évident qu'il serait irrationel d'attribuer un pareil effet à une seule decision judiciaire. Quelquefois cependant l'autorité d'un fonctionaire où d'un corps a été assez grande pour mettre hors de doute, par une seule decision, des points de droit controversés."

by private persons in certain supposed circumstances can make a law for others in similar circumstances. No one person subject to the supreme power of civil society is legally held to do, or refrain from doing, this or that act, simply because others before have, or have not, done the same; nor have any number of private individuals the power, by their example, to establish a coercive rule for another individual. Custom is juridically regarded as an effect of law, not as a cause of law. It is judicially received as an exposition of law, because that which has been generally received and acted upon by the subjects of a civil state as a rule of action is presumptively identified with the will of the supreme power of the state,[1] and is, therefore, judicially held to be reasonable or jural. The existence of the custom is judicial evidence of a rule accepted by the state for a rule of natural reason applied to certain circumstances:[2] and hence a

[1] Aristot.: Rhet., Lib. i., c. 2. Metaphy., Lib. i., c. 8. Selden: De J. Nat. etc., Heb., Lib. i., c. 6. Cicero: de Inventione, Lib. i. &c. Hobbes: De Civitate, ch. 26.
[2] Savigny: Heut. Rom. R., § 12. "So ist also die Gewohnheit das Kennzeichen des positiven Rechts, nicht dessen Entstehungsgrund." Custom is therefore the mark by which positive law is known to exist, not the cause of its existence. Tr., and refers to Puchta: "Das Gewohnheits Recht." "Every custom supposes a law," per Vaughan Ch. J. VII. Viner's Abr., 188. Statute law and common law as contrasted with Statute law, in English jurisprudence, have, therefore, the same theoretical foundation. And herein lies the essential correctness of C. J. Wilmot's saying, in 2 Wilson, 348. "The statute law is the will of the legislature in writing; the common law is nothing else but statutes worn out by time. All our law began by consent of the legislature, and whether it is now law by usage or writing is the same thing,"—and p. 350: "And statute law and common law both originally flowed from the same fountain." But compare the doctrine of Bl. Com., Introd., Sect. 3.

"Positive law," in English and American jurisprudence, is not always taken to mean statute law. Thus, in Somerset's case, Lord Mansfield says: "Positive law, which preserves its force long after the time itself from whence it was created, is erased from memory,"—but a legal rule is not a statute rule if the time of its enactment cannot be shown. So C. J. Shaw says, 18 Pick. R., 212: "by positive law in this connection may be as well understood customary law as the enactment of a statute;" and Blackstone, speaking of a provision of the common law, says, 1 Comm., 70: "now this is positive law fixed and established by custom."

Properly speaking, when custom has this general extent, its antecedent continuation is not inquired into, it is simply *law*. "A custom cannot be alleged generally within the kingdom of England; for that is common law." Co. Lit. fo., 110 b., and fo. 115 b. Sir Henry Finch, Tr., p. 77. Only particular customs require proof of their having been received for a certain length of time, to give them the force of law. Thus the authority of the Constitution of the United States rests on general custom, and much of the law of the several states not derived from England is customary law, although it has not had an existence such as is required by the law of England to give authority to a particular custom. Compare Mass. Quarterly Rev., vol. I., p. 466, On the legality of Slavery.

Of laws losing their force by desuetude. 1 Kent, 467, marg. p. 517, 7th ed., note. Dr. Irving's Introduction to the Study of the Civil Law, pp. 123—127. Woodes: Lect. prel., p. xxxiii.

custom must be tested by other indications of natural reason which, in judicial recognition, are identified with the will of the supreme power.[1]

§ 32. Not only may judicial tribunals compare together the judgments of their predecessors in applying natural law to new relations of persons and things, but they may also adopt similar comparisons made by private individuals, either oral or written, and such private writings or exposition of the law may, by force of continued judicial recognition, become a farther limitation on the discretion of subsequent tribunals.[2]

§ 33. Besides, since all states, though independent of each other, are equally possessors of the powers of society, and hold it for the same ends, they may be equally presumed to intend to conform their laws to the natural law.[3] The laws of foreign

---

[1] This testing the *legality* or *lawfulness* of a custom is a judicial act, and to be distinguished from autonomic recognition or disallowance of customs by the sovereign. Co. Lit., fo. 141, a. : "Malus usus abolendus, and every use is evil that is (as our author saith), against reason; quia in consuetudinibus non diuturnitas temporis, sed soliditas rationis est consideranda. And by this rule cited by our author at the parliament holden at Kilkenny in Ireland, (40 E. 3) Lionel, Duke of Clarence, being then the Lieutenant of that realme, the Irish customs, called then the Brehon law (for that the Irish call their judges Brehons), was wholly abolished; for that (as the parliament said) it was no law, but a lewd custom, et malus usus abolendus est. But our student must know that King John," &c. The gist of Coke's following observations appear to be—that it was by a sovereign legislative act of the Conqueror that the Brehon law was changed. In Le case de Tanistry, Davis Rep., the validity of a Brehon custom of inheritance was argued before the courts, and the usage decided to be invalid; because, according to the established judicial tests, it was no *custom* at all: the term custom having a fixed technical meaning.

[2] Kent's Comm. Lect., xxi., xxii. Falck: Jur. Ency. (French Tr.), § 10: "La *doctrine*, c'est à dire la theorie de ce qui est droit, exposée de vive voix ou par ecrit, par les savants voués à l'etude de la jurisprudence, devrait, d'apres sa nature, être seulement un moyen auxilliaire pour apprendre à connaitre le droit en vigueur; cependant elle est devenue, à plusieurs égards, une véritable source du droit. La literature juridique en particulier a exercée, à certaines époques, comme le montrent toutes les histoires du droit, une si grande influence, que beaucoup d'ouvrages de jurisprudence ont obtenu formellement force de loi. Mais, il faut le dire, c'est là un abus veritable, qui n'a pas d'autre motif que la paresse d'esprit, ou la foi à l'autorité."
Dig., Lib. I., Tit. ii., c. 2, § 12. Ita in civitate nostra, aut jure, id est lege, constituitur, aut est proprium jus civile, quod sine scripto in sola prudentum interpretatione consistit.
Grotius, B. et P., Lib. I., c. i., § 14. Savigny, on the vocation of our age for legislation and jurisprudence, Hayward's Transl., pp. 28, 29, 30. Rum on Legal Judgment, ch. 18, sect. 5. Reddie: Law of Marit. Com., p. 438.
This authority of private jurists must depend upon some juridical recognition: compare Bacon: de Aug. Sci., Lib. viii., c. 3, § 10. De Justitia Universali, App., 72—92. Though in the Roman system, an intrinsic authority seems to have been attributed to the Responsa Prudentum: see Savigny: Heut. R. R., B. I., c. 3, §§ 14, 26. Butler's Horæ Juridicæ, Essay, Roman Law. De Ferriere: Hist. of Roman Law, ch. ix.

[3] Heffter: Europäisches Völkerrecht, p. 22, speaks of a class or school of publicists

states (i. e. their municipal, or, more correctly, their national laws), whether arising from positive legislation, or from the judgment of their tribunals, applying the law of natural reason, may also be received by the tribunals of any one state as an exposition of the law of nature, where its own positive legislation or judicial interpretation of natural law does not afford sufficient guidance.[1]

§ 34. And when any principles or rules of action have been so long and so generally recognized among many nations that they have been historically known as the *law of nations*, or *universal* principles forming the subject of a general or universal jurisprudence, they will, for the same reason, which here applies still more forcibly, be presumed to conform to natural reason or natural law;[2] and be judicially received as the presumptive will of

---

who find the natural law of jurisprudence in the expressed will of states, by assuming that they have intended to do justice—" Das Wollen der Gerechtigkeit in den Willen der Nationen eingeschlossen betrachten."

[1] Sir Henry Finch: Treatise on the Common Law, p. 6. Ram: Legal Judgment, p. 69—71, 76. Marshall: on Ins., Prelim. Disc. p. 24. Reddie's Inq. Elem. &c., p. 196. "Finally, in the exposition of common law, judges have been accustomed to look to the legal systems and judicial experience of other nations, if not as standards, or imperative sources of the law, at least as affording practical guides by which they may be led to decide aright, &c." On this principle, the Roman law is referred to in English and American jurisprudence. Wood's Inst., Introd: Spence: Equity Jurisd. of Court of Ch., vol. i., 119, 122-3. 5 Bingham, 167. Long's Discourses, passim; Reddie's Hist. View of Marit. Com., pp. 428. 438. Cushing's Roman Law, §§ 250, 333, 4, 5. Butler's Horæ Juridicæ, p. 60. So also the Canon Law, even in Protestant countries, Hor. Jurid. p. 122.

In the tribunals of Continental Europe, the Roman law has so long been received on this principle, that it is looked upon by many of the civilians, as being in and of itself an authoritative exposition of natural reason. In their language—Valet pro ratione, non pro introducto jure. Non habet vim legis, sed rationis. Servatur ubique jus Romanum, non ratione imperii, sed rationis imperio.

[2] Savigny: Heut. R. R., B. i., c. 3, § 22. Grotius: B. et P., Lib. i., 12, 2. Cic. i., Tusc. Ep., 117—" In omni re consensio omnium gentium jus naturæ putanda est."

2 Bla. Comm., 11, note by Christian. "I know no other criterion by which we can determine any rule or obligation to be founded in nature than by its universality, and by inquiring whether it has not in all countries and ages been agreeable to the feelings, affections, and reason of mankind."

Doctor and Student, p. 63. *Doct.* "Therefore it seemeth that contracts be grounded upon the law of reason, or at least upon the law that is called *jus gentium*;" and p. 176: *Stud.* "First, it is to be understood that contracts be grounded upon a custom of the realm, and by the law that is called *jus gentium*, and not directly by the law of reason."

It is this ascertained standard which apparently Pothier, in Treatise on Obligations, 15, intends by "pure natural right." And see definition of *Maxims*, in Ram: Legal Judgment, p. 14, and the citations.

Whatever principle a tribunal may admit to be a principle of universal jurisprudence must be taken to be received in the national law which that tribunal is appointed to administer. (Suarez: De Leg. et Deo Legisl., Lib. ii., c. 19, § 2—6.)

the state: and though these principles must originally have acquired that character of universality from the independent legislative wills of single states, yet, when they have acquired that historical character, they may be judicially received by the tribunals of any one state as an *independent* indication of natural law, presumed, from the fact of being received in universal jurisprudence or for universal jurisprudence, to be adopted as *a priori* principles by that national power whose juridical will the tribunal is intended to execute.

§ 35. When the natural law, or law of natural reason has thus been judicially interpreted, and thus made a part of the *positive* law of any one state or nation,[1] (i. e. positive in respect to

---

The tribunal refers to the historical indicia of this universal jurisprudence as being one of the criteria of the legislative will of the state, which is to be juridically applied. In the Roman jurisprudence, no principle was ascribed to the *jus gentium*, which was not included in the civil law (i. e., national law) of Rome. Comp. Fœlix : Droit International Privé, § 5. Reddie's Inq. El. &c., p. 26, and see *post* ch. ii., and iv.

But for an opposite theory of natural law in Jurisprudence, see Hoffman's Legal Outlines, sect. viii.

Smith's Merc. Law, p. 2. Speaking of the comparative utility of historical researches in the law of real estate and mercantile law :—" Our mercantile law, on the contrary, is wholly founded on considerations of utility ; and though many of its rules are derived from the institutions of ancient times and distant countries, still is their introduction into our system owing, not to a blind respect for their origin, but to an enlightened sense of their propriety. No one, unless acquainted with their feudal source, could assign any reason for those rules which respect fines, escheats, or recoveries ; but it is not necessary, for the purpose of enabling the reader to see the justice and good sense of the law of general average, to show him that it formed part of the maritime code of the ancient Rhodians. At the same time, it cannot be denied that the history of our commercial law is a subject of great interest and rational curiosity, &c."

Here is an example of a very common misapprehension of the origin of law in general, and particularly of the derivation of that branch called mercantile law. The author misapprehends the reason why the rule of general average has the force of law in cases of maritime losses. It is not law *because* agreeable to justice and good sense. If it were not that the maritime nations of Europe (the Rhodians being the first, perhaps, as matter of history) had actually given it the binding force of a law within their several jurisdictions, the judges of English courts would have had no right to apply it in enforcing a contribution. If the judges of our courts should to-morrow be of opinion that the rule hitherto pursued is not "agreeable to justice and good sense," they might—according to the author's argument—decline to apply it any longer.

And see another instance in Abbott on Shipping, Preface to the First Edition ; where the author gives the *reasons* for referring to the maritime code of Louis XIV., as authority for English tribunals; and see Benedict's Admiralty Pr., § 5. Duer, on Insur., p. 2. Emerigon, c. i., § 6, note, by English editor. That the Roman tribunal made judicial reference to the laws of the Rhodians on the ground of its being an existing foreign law, see Peckius : De Re Nautica, Ad leg. Rh. De Jactu. *Rubrica.*

[1] Vinnius Comm., Lib. i., Tit. 2, § 1. "'Vocaturque jus civile.'—In specie nimirum, nam jus civile sumptum pro eo jure quo in universum civitas utitur, etiam jus naturale et gentium, quatenus receptum est, comprehendit ; eoque sensu, obligationes, quæ ex contractibus juris gentium descendunt, dicuntur civiles : licet a legislatore

its authority, *v. ante*, § 17,) it may still be distinguished as the unwritten law, the customary law, the common law of the land.¹

civili nihil habeant præter approbationem, (§ 1, inf. de oblig.) Hoc igitur dicitur civile a causa efficiente, quæ est voluntas alicujus civitatis aut ejus qui jus legis ferendæ in ea habet, non communis gentium aut naturalis ratio. Ab Aristotele legitimum dicitur: vulgo positivum."

¹ Even under a written code, this part of the law must continue. See, as to the recognition of this, under the French Code, Savigny: Vocation of our Age, &c. Hayward's Tr., p. 90. Also, Duponceau on Jurisd., p. 106. Reddie's Inq. Elem. &c., pp. 199—202.

In this description of the mode in which positive law becomes judicially ascertained, there is no distinction of any part of the law which can be distinguished from the rest as *equity*, or as an equitable rule of action. The distinction which exists in English and American jurisprudence between *law* and *equity* is not in the nature of the rule, but in the means by which it is enforced. " In England and America Equity, in the technical legal sense of that term, as opposed to or distinct from the common law, is in reality as much as the common law, customary or judiciary law; a part of the general law of the realm." Reddie: Inq. Elem., p. 124. Blac. Comm., 3, c. 27, p. 432. Every rule of action which the supreme power in England or America enforces as law is equally jural—equally a *lex juris*. The distinction here is one of jurisdiction, or of remedy—the application of the rule of action, arising from the authority allowed to judicial precedent, and a consequence of that supremacy of law as opposed to arbitrary discretion, which is a characteristic of " Anglican liberty." (For the use of this term, see Lieber: Civil Liberty and Self Government, vol. i., ch. v.) The occasion given to a common misconception of the nature of positive law by the existence of an " Equity Jurisprudence," may excuse an attempt to set this forth in the limits of a note.

The rule of action to which the state gives the authority of law must be enforced or vindicated by the state, if it is to be efficacious in accomplishing the object of the state, i. e., justice. This can only be done by judicial remedies. In a state where precedents have great force as an indication of the will of the supreme power, the remedy which has been applied to enforce the rule of action becomes itself a precedent, that is, it becomes a rule or law of remedy, and thus the efficacy of a rule of action becomes limited to circumstances in which only a remedy has been before applied. The same effect would take place if the remedial mode of enforcing the rule of action were prescribed by statute.

The rule of action will thus, in course of time, fail in many instances of its original intention, i. e., justice: because new circumstances of disobedience to the rule will occur, differing from those to which the known law of remedy applies. The state must, therefore, in order to effect its intention, i. e., justice, either directly prescribe a remedy in those new circumstances, or direct that its tribunals should go beyond precedent in the law of remedy, and enforce the rule of action according to its original intention. The state may establish a *separate tribunal* with power to carry out the rule of action beyond the remedy given by the precedents of existing tribunals.

In course of time, the remedy given by the new court becomes also a precedent; and has a law of its own. There are thus two systems of remedy intended to carry out one and the same law of right. In English and American jurisprudence, this double system of remedy exists. *Equity* is not a different rule of action from *law*; it is a law of remedy.

Papers read before the Juridical Society, Vol. i., Part I., 1855. London: Stevens & Norton. Inaugural Address by Sir R. Bethell, S. G., M.P., p. 3—" And the rules and maxims of the common law were so broad and comprehensive, that they admitted of being made the basis of an enlarged system of jurisprudence. A portion of the statute of Westminster the second (13 Edw. I.) was passed with a view of effecting this object, and of expanding the maxims of the common law, so as to render it applicable to the exigencies of an advancing state of society. For this purpose, new writs were directed to be framed, as new occasions for remedial justice presented themselves; and if this had been fully acted on, the law of England might have been ma-

It is this which constitutes the common law in the jurisprudence of England and America, when distinguished from statute law.[1]

§ 36. This recognition and adoption of the natural law occurs in international as well as in municipal (national) law.

As was before said, each nation being independent of other nations, whatever is enforced by its own tribunals as law rests upon its own authority, or is identified, in respect to its authority, with the municipal law of that state. International law, though differing from municipal law in the objects or relations which it affects, does not, as administered by its tribunals, rest on any other authority than the state itself: it is then a part of the municipal (national) law; being then distinguished from other portions of the municipal law only by its application to persons, or as one personal law is distinguished from another.[2] Whatever rules the tribunal may administer as international law, are

---

tured into a uniform and comprehensive system. For it was justly observed by one of the judges in the reign of Henry the Sixth, that if actions on the case had been allowed by courts of law as often as occasion required, the writ of subpœna would have been unnecessary; or, in other words, there would have been no distinctions between courts of law and courts of equity, and the whole of the present jurisdiction of the court of chancery, would have been part of the ordinary jurisdiction of courts of law."

See on this point, Story; Equity Jurisprudence, vol. I. Bacon: Advanc. Learn., B. viii., c. 3, of Univ. Just. Aphorisms, 22 to 46. Ram on Legal Judgment, ch. ii., and authorities; also, Am. Jurist, vol. xvii., p. 253, on reform in remedial law. D'Aguesseau: Œuvres, Tom. i., p. 209. Lessee of Livingston *v.* Moore and others, 7 Peter's R., p. 547. Butler's Horæ Juridicæ, p. 44—46.

In the states of Continental Europe, where the administration of justice is on the model of the Roman law, judicial tribunals are less fettered by judicial precedent, and have always had a greater latitude in applying the rule of action. The judicial officer has in practice a large share of administrative power. His power to make law for future cases is less than that of judges under the English system; but his autonomous or discretionary power over the case in hand is far greater. Hence the rights of individuals depend less on pre-existent law, and more on arbitrary discretion.

[1] Sir H. Finch: Treatise, p. 74. Sims' Case, 7 Cushing R., p. 313. Shaw, C. J., using the term *positive law*:—" and this may be mere customary law, as well as the enactment of a statute. The term 'positive law,' in this sense, may be understood to designate those rules established by long and tacit acquiescence, or by the legislative act of any state, and which derive their force and effect, as law from such acquiescence and legislative enactment, and are acted upon as such, whether conformable to the dictates of natural justice or otherwise." And comp. Neal *v.* Farmer, 9 Georgia R., 581.

Ram, on Judgment, ch. ii. Savigny: Heut. R. R., § 18. Reddie's Inq. Elem. &c., p. 238—252,—a description of the establishment of municipal (national) law, abridged from Savigny.

Bentham: Princ. Morals and Legisl., pref., xiii. "Common law, as it styles itself in England; judiciary law, as it might more aptly be styled everywhere," &c. Compare Ency. Am., vol. vii., Appendix, LAW, &c., by Story.

Co. Lit., fo. 11., a. An enumeration of the "proofs and arguments of the common law," drawn from twenty several fountains or places; common law being taken in the limited sense; because in the same place *communis lex Angliæ* is included *en la ley*.

[2] See *post*, § 53.

derived by it in the same manner as municipal law; viz. firstly, from the positive legislation of the state in reference to relations which are international in their character; that is, relations arising out of the existence of foreign states, and from the recognition of their authority to give laws and hold jurisdiction over persons and things. Such legislation must be recognized by the tribunal on the authority of the state alone to which it belongs, whether it be made by the state singly, or jointly with other states, in the form of treaties and agreements. Secondly: from the recognition of natural law by such criteria or expositions of that law, applied to the same international relations, as may be supposed to be adopted by the state to which the tribunal belongs, and whose will it executes in the administration of international law as well as of the municipal: and these are the same as are adopted in ascertaining the municipal law—decisions of preceding tribunals having the same national authority, the writings of private jurists, and the laws and decisions and customs of all other states;[1] comprehending herein, also, the recognition of universal jurisprudence, the science of a *law of nations* historically known: which recognition by judicial tribunals is particularly manifest and necessary in the administration of private international law, as will be shown in the following chapter. International law, thus applied by the *judicial tribunals* of any state, is only to be distinguished from the municipal law of that state in the *nature of the relations* which it affects; it is identified with it in respect to its *authority* over all persons within the jurisdiction of the state.[2]

---

[1] Grotius : B. et P. Proleg., § 40, Lib. I., c. i., § 12, 14. I. Kent's Comm., 18, 19. Reddie : Hist. View L. of Marit. Com., 26, 27, 426, 429. Hoffman's Course of Legal Study, vol. i., p. 415–16. Burge : Col. and For. Law, vol. i., xvi. Ram, on Legal Judgment, p. 94. Phillimore : Internat. L., p. 61.

It is only civilized nations, or those of a certain kind of culture, that are thus recognized by their several tribunals as the sources of universal jurisprudence. See Selden : De J. Nat. &c., Lib. i., c. vi., who designates them as "*gentes moratiores*," in the language of Grotius : B. et P., Lib. i., 12, 2. Phillimore : Int. L., c. iii. Heffter designates his work—Das Heutige *Europäische* Völkerrecht.

This discrimination between different nations as sources of jural rules, is not an *a priori* assumption by the tribunal making it. It is rather a part of the customary law of the state whose will the tribunal is bound to apply. This act of a judicial tribunal must not be confounded with the sovereign *legislative* act of a state in adopting a foreign law, as when in the XII. tables, the Romans adopted some of the laws of Greece. Dig. L. I., Tit. 2, c. 2, § 4 ; "peterentur leges a Græcis civitatibus."

[2] This point is more fully considered in the second chapter.

§ 37. From the conditions necessary to the existence of a relation between states, or from the fact that though composed of natural persons, each subject to the power of society, they have a distinct existence and power of action in respect to each other, as well as in respect to private individuals, any rule which would decide on the relations of states, as such, towards each other, and maintain their correlative rights and duties, would be an international law. But from the nature of states and their mutual independence, there is no such rule, taking the word *law* in the strict sense; and the application of such a rule or law could not be made by the judicial tribunals of any state or nation. A coercive determination of these rights and obligations can be expected only from the autonomic force of the parties to whom this law may attribute them.

But from the reciprocal assertion and acknowledgment which all states or nations have in fact made of principles of natural reason, or from that course of practice which is supposed to be founded on a reciprocal reference to such principles in their relations with each other, and from the consideration actually allowed to the ethical views of some private authors in reference to such national practice, an exposition of natural law has arisen, which corresponds with the common law, or judicially ascertained municipal (national) law of any one state, having in practice the character of a rule of action for states; determining their relations to each other, and the correlative rights and obligations of each, though there is no tribunal to decide between them in its application;—that is, no tribunal which can enforce the rights and obligations, arising under it, in particular cases.[1]

§ 38. Rules thus recognized form a part of universal jurisprudence, (*law of nations* in that sense,) to which states or nations reciprocally refer as to an international law having an existence

---

[1] Even Mr. Reddie, who distinguishes the existence of a universal jurisprudence operating as part of the coercive private law of each several nation, seems to hold that there is a law derived in the same manner, and operating on the state as a political person, having the *same kind* of authority. See Inquiries Elem. &c., 2d ed., p. 456, and Inq. in International Law, 2d ed., 439, 456.

Wheaton, in his El. of International Law, § 10, cites Heffter as taking the same view; but in the last ed. of Das Europäische Völkerrecht der Gegenwart, Berlin, 1855, p. 2, n. 2, the latter author says that Mr. Wheaton has misconceived his meaning.

independent of their several juridical assent. In its *origin*, this law, of which nations are then taken to be the subjects, is identified with the law applied by judicial tribunals as an interpretation of the law of natural reason between private persons, in both municipal (internal) and international law,—the *law of nations*, in the sense of private law judicially recognised because existing among all nations. And though it is *a law* for those nations only in the imperfect sense of the word, it may be called a part of *positive* law, or be included in jurisprudence—the science of positive law, when the term *positive* is used not to indicate the coercive quality, but the quality of being an ascertained rule,—a rule having an *objective* existence independently of the *subjective* conception of any one state or nation, or of any private person or persons ; a rule which is not necessarily the true law of nature or of natural right, but that which many states have agreed in applying for such.[1] As such it is referred to by sovereign nations for public law, and is enforced by judicial tribunals for private law, being binding on those tribunals until contravened or disallowed by the several juridical action of the states to which they belong, or for which they exercise the judicial function.

§ 39. It is always consistent for sovereign powers to reconsider their own previous judgment in respect to any application of the law of nature. This may be done by single sovereignties in either division of the municipal (internal) law, constituting, in private law, social change or reform,[2] and in public law, civil or political change or revolution : in either of which forms the

---

[1] The controversial writings of publicists on these questions of definition are noted in all the treatises on international public law. Though it may be difficult to estimate the actual influence of professed metaphysicians on these subjects, (compare Wheaton : Hist. of the Law of Nations, p. 749, and Heffter : Europ. Völkerr., § 9,) it is probable that the distinctions made by Kant, Fichte and Hegel, in their juristical writings, have led to a greater accuracy of expression on these topics. It is worthy of notice that the positions taken by some later authors correspond in a remarkable degree with those of Suarez the Jesuit, one of the earliest writers. That attention to them has been renewed is shown by the proposal of M. Greuse, of Brussels, to republish the entire works of Suarez.

[2] B. Constant: Cours de Politique, Œuvres, Tom. i., p. 174, n. "Souvent les dépositaires du pouvoir sont partis du principe que la justice existait avant les lois, pour soumettre les individus à des lois rétroactives, ou pour les priver du bénéfice des lois existantes ; couvrant de la sorte d'un feint respect pour la justice la plus révoltante des iniquités. Tant il importe sur les objets de ce genre, de se garder d'axiomes non définis

change may be either gradual or sudden, peaceful or violent.[1]

Or this reconsideration may be made by sovereign national powers in international law ; either in that law which each state applies by its own tribunals to persons in international relations, for the private international law, or those reciprocal rules of intercourse, which, as the parties to be governed by the rule, they may mutually adopt for public international law, (in the imperfect sense of a law.) Both which divisions of international law have been constantly changed and extended during the time of recorded history, according to altered views of natural equity.

Universal jurisprudence or the *law of nations*, whether taken to be a rule determining the relations of states or of private persons, being thus a consequence of the juridical action of states or nations, is always liable to changes, which (from the *a priori* principle before stated, viz. that the legislative action of states is always juridical or jural, that is conformed to natural reason) must be taken to be progress or improvement.[2]

§ 40. Under the preceding view of the nature and extent of the law, every action and relation which is the subject of jurisprudence may be taken to be determined either by international or by municipal (national) law.

The rights of persons, though all *relative* in respect to other persons owing or bound to corresponding obligations, may be distinguished as rights in correspondence with obligations on the part of the community at large, or as rights correspondent to obligations on the part of particular persons.[3]

---

[1] Revolution is resistance against the *legal* possessor of sovereign power. But it is founded on the assertion of a share of sovereignty, or right of supreme control, in the revolutionist, (a right above *law*,) and in case of success, the change, whether ethically rightful or not, becomes *lawful*, by being the act of the actual sovereign.

[2] Suarez: de Legib. et Deo Legisl., ch. 20, § 6, 8. Doctor and Student, p. 63: "For though the law called *jus gentium* be much necessary for the people, yet it may be changed."

Whewell: El. Mor. and Pol., § 1143. "The law of nations, including in this international law, is subject to the conditions of which we have already spoken as belonging to the law of any one nation. It is capable of progressive standards: it is fixed for a given time, and obligatory while it is fixed: but it must acknowledge the authority of morality, and must, in order to conform to the moral nature of man, become constantly more and more moral. The progress of international law in this respect is more slow and irregular than that of a well guided national law, &c." And compare Savigny's Vocation of our age for Legislation and Jurisprudence, Hayward's Translation, p. 134.

[3] Reddie's Inquiries Elem. &c., p. 171. See citation, *ante*, page 20, note: "But

INDIVIDUAL AND RELATIVE RIGHTS. 37

The first class may be called *individual* rights, as belonging to persons each necessarily or absolutely recognized before the law as individual members of society. The individual rights of persons, (called by Blackstone, *absolute*,) have ordinarily been taken to be three, denominated: the right of personal liberty; the right of personal security; and the right of property.[1]

The second class may be called *relative* rights, as belonging to persons in consequence of a relation established between them and others, not necessarily arising from their being individual members of the community.

These relative rights have been classed as the rights of parent and child; of husband and wife; of master and servant.

Both individual and relative rights, considered with reference to the persons to whom they are attributed, may be called private rights; while, in view of their existence in relation to the supreme power of society or the state, and the persons of whom it is composed, they may also be termed civil and public rights.

§ 41. From the nature of law, in its ordinary sense, including the idea of inferiority and subjection, corresponding with superiority and authority, the term *a right* implies a *liberty* in the person to whom the right is attributed; *jus est facultas agendi*. The idea of *freedom* associated with the idea of *law*, or legal freedom, as the *condition* of a person, consists in the

---

though rights and obligations are in reality and correctly, the relations of individual persons to other individuals, they are plainly correlative terms. And it is manifest, in the first place, that they may exist between any one individual, or a definite number of individuals, and all other individuals generally and indefinitely, the right being positive against all others, *adversus omnes*, and the obligation on all others being only negative. Or they may exist between particular individuals, and instead of being *adversus omnes*, directed against all other individuals indefinitely, may exist or be directed only against one or more particular individuals, who are under corresponding obligation, not merely negative not to interfere, but positive to do, or bear, or suffer something for the behoof of the person having the right." And see Austin: Prov. of Jurisp., Appendix, xxiv., xxv., definitions of rights *in rem* and in personam. Also, Mackeldey: Compend. Mod. Civil Law, Introd., §§ 15, 16.

[1] Dr. Lieber denominates such rights *primordial*. Pol. Eth., vol. i., p. 218. Civil Lib. and Self Gov., vol. i., p. 52. The terms absolute or primordial convey the idea of rights anterior or independent of positive law as herein before defined: rights existing under some independent law of nature: which, as before shown, has no existence, —no judicial recognition in jurisprudence, as independent of positive law. *Primordial* is a term liable to the same objections which Dr. Lieber advances against the term *absolute* in the place referred to. He also uses the term *individual* as a synonym. P. E., vol. i., p. 402: "We speak of individual primordial rights." *Droits individuels* is a common term in this sense with the French jurists. Ahrens: Naturrecht, p. 160. speaks of *Individuellen Rechte*.

possession of legal rights of action, or in that liberty which is allowed by law.

Where liberty is attributed to a being existing under conditions over which it has no control, it cannot be defined except with reference to those conditions, or laws in the secondary sense of the word law. And when attributed to a moral being governed by rules of action, (laws in the primary sense,) liberty can be defined only by stating the source, authority, and extent of those laws, as well as their object, or the direct effect of their injunctions.

§ 42. The definition of liberty, when attributed to individual members of a state or political body, has been a problem for publicists.[1] There are evidently two modes in which such liberty may be conceived of. In one, liberty is determined by ethical considerations, or as that freedom of action which *ought* —in accordance with the nature of man—to be the effect of the laws of a political state. This is a *subjective* apprehension of liberty, because the moral judgment of the concipient is the highest criterion of its real nature, and the test of its very existence.

In the alternative mode of conception, liberty is the object of a legal apprehension. That is, it is viewed as that actual degree of freedom which *exists*, or is allowed to the individual member of the civil state under the power of society and the unalterable conditions of human existence. Its conception is entirely independent of the moral sense of the concipient, and may be said to be the *objective* apprehension.

Liberty, in the first named aspect, is a subject of that science which relates to that necessary condition of man's existence as a moral being; and belongs to the province of political ethics. It is in the last described point of view that it becomes a topic of jurisprudence, in the sense herein before given to that term, viz. the science of positive law. No definition of liberty, when thus regarded, can be given but by defining it as the effect of the law of some state or nation, and without describing the law of some state or independent political society.[2]

---

[1] See Lieber: On Civil Liberty and Self Government, ch. ii., and the citations.
[2] Compare Dr. Lieber: Civil Liberty and Self Government, ch. iv., v. Therefore,

§ 43. Since the nature of a legal right implies a duty or obligation as a correspondent constituent of some relation between persons, that obligation or duty may be considered as the opposite of a liberty : or, the duties made obligatory upon a person by law may be said to constitute a *condition* opposed to legal freedom. As the *condition of freedom* in this sense is indefinite, and is determined according to the nature and extent of the rights given by the law, so is all that is in this manner opposed to it determined by the nature and extent of the obligations or duties imposed by the law.

When a state of freedom, in this sense, is attributed to any subject, a power of choice and action is, by the signification of the words, necessarily supposed to exist in that subject, in the absence of law limiting or defining that freedom. According to the use of words, freedom cannot be predicated of anything which is without powers of choice and action. Therefore, according to the definition of a *person* in jurisprudence, (*ante* § 21,) freedom can be attributed to *persons* only. The same may be said of any state or condition opposite to freedom ; only *persons*, as having the power of choice and action in the absence of restraint, can be said to be *bound* by law, (in the primary sense;) and, therefore, *bondage*, as expressing a condition opposite to freedom, can be properly ascribed to *persons* only.

§ 44. The individual and relative rights of persons are capable, under the supreme power of the state, of such various modification between the extremes which constitute on the one hand a state of license, and on the other, the extremity of coercion which is physically possible, that the laws of freedom and bondage, as constituting opposite conditions of legal *persons*, might be considered under the description of these various rights and their corresponding obligations, as they exist under municipal (national) and international law.

a presumption in favor of the personal liberty of any private person is not a necessary principle in jurisprudence. There may be in some states a constant legal presumption against the freedom of certain persons, and hence a presumption that some other person must have over them a right of control. The law, in resting on the authority of civil society, can derive no rules of action, and therefore no rights or obligations, from that state of nature which some authors have supposed to have existed anterior to civil society or the state. The *natural* freedom of man is known in jurisprudence only so ar as it is the result either of laws in the secondary sense—conditions of things, or has been acknowledged and realized in the rules of natural reason which are identified with positive law.

But since the *non*-possession of legal rights may be said to be the opposite of freedom, and since *things*, in the idea of the law (being only the objects of action, and never the subjects of rights) can have no legal rights, every object which the law contemplates as a thing, may, by a somewhat loose use of language, be said to be in a legal condition opposed in the farthest degree to freedom. Positive law being necessarily understood to be a rule of action for mankind,[1] it might from this alone be inferred that the law attributes capacity for choice and action, or personality, to all men; or that the legal personality of all men is to be taken as a necessary or natural first principle of all law resting on the authority of society, or of the states holding the powers of society. But in accordance with the proposition that there is no other *legal* criterion of natural law than such as is sanctioned or adopted by the state, there is room in the jurisprudence of every country for an inquiry into the absoluteness or extent of such legal recognition of mankind as persons,[2] or for the question, whether some part of mankind may be legally wanting in the character of personality, distinguishing them from things, and may be in legal relations, *things;*—only the objects of the rights of persons, and never the subjects of rights.[3]

[1] Dig. L. I. Tit. 5, § 2. Quum igitur omne jus hominum causa constitutum sit,—Inst. L. I. Tit. 2. § 12—parum est jus nosse, si personæ, quarum causa constitutum est, ignorentur.

[2] Thibaut : Syst. d. Pand. Rechts.—Vol. I. § 118. *Tr:* "The third topic which is to be considered in relation to rights and obligations is their subject, that is to say, the person who has the capacity or obligation. And here the question directly arises: who can be the subject of a right,—either in respect to the nature of the thing (natural capacity for rights) or in respect to the precepts of positive law, (civil capacity for rights.) He who in any respect is considered as the subject of a right, is to that extent denominated a *person;* particularly considered as the subject of civil rights. On the other hand, that is called a *thing* which constitutes the opposite of a person : civil capacity for rights is what the Romans call *status* or *caput*. The moderns give it the name of *status civilis*, as consisting of all the capacities attributed by the laws, to which particular rights are attached; the natural capacity for rights on the other hand, as consisting of physical capacities which are followed by particular relations, is called by them *status naturalis.*" Compare Lindley's Transl. § 101. Mackeldey's Comp. by Kaufmann, § 116, 117. Ahrens' Naturrecht, p. 83, 84, also published in French.

Falck : Jurist. Encyc. § 27. French Tr. " On peut considérer comme une introduction générale la théorie du *Status*, où l'on résout la question de savoir jusqu'à quel point l'état a reconnu la capacité juridique aux êtres humains qui vivent sous sa protection, de manière qu'en leur en supposant la possibilité physique, ils puissent entrer dans certains rapports de droit et y persister. Ce point était beaucoup plus important dans l'ancien droit, que dans le droit actuel; car nous ne connaissons guère aujourd'hui d'autres causes d'exclusions des rapports juridiques, que celles qui les rendent physiquement impossibles."

[3] In the Roman law the condition of all natural persons as subjects of law was de-

If the law can be supposed to attribute the *legal* character of a thing to that which has a *natural* capacity for choice and action, or which is a *natural person*, the legal condition of that natural person would not be explained by the term *bondage* as above defined; since that presupposes a recognition by the law of a capacity to act or not to act, or of the personality of that which is legally *bound*. That condition would be legally included under the law of things, or of the rights of persons in respect to things: property, or possession and control by legal persons, being the essential legal attribute of a natural person who can appear in legal relations only as the object of rights, while the attribution of legal personality, by implying capacity for choice and action, recognizes a legal capacity for individual and relative rights, and makes every condition of the person which may be opposed to freedom, to consist in *obligations* under relations to other persons. But where the law admits the contradiction of recognizing a natural capacity for choice and action, and at the same time attributing that incapacity for rights which belongs to the nature of a *thing*, this species of bondage would require a legal name distinguishing the subject from natural things and from legal persons.[1] Under systems of law where this anomalous condition has been known, it has been included under the general terms bondage or slavery, and is sometimes more definitively known as chattel bondage or chattel slavery.[2]

---

scribed under the name of *caput* or *status*, and divided into three parts; or rather described as existing under either one, two, or three conditions, each called *status* or *caput*, under each of which the condition of the individual might be variously affected. These were called *libertas, civitas, familia*. The law of the *status libertatis* however comprised the distinction between a personal condition as *liber* or freeman and the chattel condition of a *servus* or slave; and the law of the *status*, in its most general sense, may be taken as the Roman phrase for the law of freedom and of bondage. For the sake of a convenient term, it will be here sometimes used to designate the legal condition of a private person, considered under the American law affecting personal condition in these respects. See Thibaut, by Lindley, § 106. Mackeldey, by Kaufman, §§ 119, 120, 121.

[1] Novel. Theod., Tit. 17, "Servos... quasi nec personam habentes."

[2] Austin: Prov. Jur., p. 279, note. "From the assumed inconsistency of slavery with the law of God, or nature, it is not unfrequently inferred by fanatical enemies of the institution that the master has no right, or cannot have a right, to the slave. If they said that his right is pernicious, and that therefore he ought not to have it, they would speak to the purpose. But to dispute the existence, or the possibility of the right, is to talk absurdly. For in every age, and in almost every nation, the right has been given by positive law; whilst that pernicious disposition of positive law has been backed by the positive morality of the free, or master classes." "Positive law," according to this author's definition, which includes every rule that is *law*, not legislative enactment merely.

SLAVERY DEFINED.

§ 45. The idea of chattel slavery, in the strict legal sense, is definite and easily conceived. When the term slavery is used to express the condition of a *legal person*, one having a recognized capacity for rights and duties, it may be attributed to various conditions of obligation on the part of one person opposed to the conditions of privilege on the part of others. Chattel slavery may exist under restrictions by municipal law on the power of the master, in view of the interests of society, without vesting the rights of a legal person in the slave.[1] The person held in slavery may continue to have the character of property, in the eye of the law, in states wherein, under the influence of public opinion or other moral causes, protection is in practice ensured to the slave as a natural person, unknown to other communities wherein the law upon which the relation rests is the same in judicial apprehension. By a greater or less legal recognition of rights in the slave, and of corresponding duties on the part of the master or owner, the fundamental character of that condition may be changed, and the property recognized by the law be made to consist in the right of one person to the labor or services of another. Every recognition of rights in the slave, independent of the will of the owner or master, which is made by the state to which he is subject, diminishes in some degree the essence of that slavery by changing it into a relation between legal persons.

§ 46. The term slavery has been popularly applied to various forms of servitude or bondage, instituted under municipal law. But in its general legal acceptation it may be defined as that condition of a natural person, in which, by the operation of law, the application of his physical and mental powers depends, as far as possible, upon the will of another who is himself subject to the supreme power of the state,[2] and in which he is incapable, in the view of the law, of acquiring or holding property, and of sustaining those relations out of which *relative* rights, as herein before defined (§ 40) proceed, except as the agent or instrument

---

[1] Savigny: Heut. R. R., B. ii., c. 2, § 65.
[2] But the legal condition of slavery may exist, even though the person to whom it is ascribed is not the bondman, or property of any particular person, or master. See Savigny: Heut. R. R., B. ii., c. 1, § 55, note, a), c. 2, § 65, for illustrations under the Roman law.

SLAVERY DEFINED.

of another. In slavery, strictly so called, the supreme power of the state, in ignoring the personality of the slave, ignores his capacity for moral action, and commits the control of his conduct as a moral agent, to the master,[1] together with the power of transferring his authority to another. So far as it may hold the master and slave, as individuals, morally responsible to the state in their mutual relation, it so far recognizes the personality of the slave, and changes the property into a relation between persons.

§ 47. It is evident that there may be political or economical regulations in a civil state which, while not interfering directly with the freedom or security of the person, or denying the abstract right of any to the acquisition or enjoyment of property, may yet, in view of public or of partial interests, by prohibition of certain modes of action, or by the grant of superior privileges to others, so obstruct the industry of some classes of persons and repress their moral and physical energies, as to make their actual condition in the social scale lower than that of others living under the control of a private master who is guided in its exercise by wisdom and benevolence.

Municipal laws may so operate in disabling certain classes or races in a nation, with respect to their private or public relations, as to reduce them to a species of dependence upon more privileged classes deserving, in a general sense, the name of slavery or bondage.[2] The distinction of these cases from slavery, properly so called, lies in the legal view of the slave or of his labor as private property, and the greater or less denial of his personality, making the disposal of his person and labor to depend

---

[1] Menander *apud* Stobœus: Florileg lx., 34.

'Εμοὶ πόλις ἐστι καὶ καταφυγὴ καὶ νόμος
Καὶ τοῦ δικαίου τοῦ τ'ἀδίκου παντὸς κριτὴς
'Ο δεσπότης. Πρὸς τοῦτον ἕνα δεῖ ζῆν ἐμέ.

Spinoza: Tr. Theol. Pol., c. xvi. "Si finis actionis non est ipsius agentis sed imperantis utilitas, tum agens servus est, et sibi inutilis."

[2] For illustrations of the variety of meaning attached to liberty and slavery, see 20 Howell, State Trials, Somerset's case, p. 14, note of English editor, sneering at the boasts of the French lawyers in the negro case, 13th vol. of Causes Celebres, (temp. Louis XV.,) p. 492, ed. 1747. And compare Chancellor Harper's Essay, p. 23. See Molyneux: Case of Ireland, by Almon, p. 169. "I have no other notion of slavery but being bound by a law to which I do not consent." In defining liberty, Dig. Lib. i., De statu hominum, Inst., Lib. i., Tit. 3, De jure personarum,—Libertas est naturalis facultas ejus, quod cuique facere libet, nisi si quid vi, aut jure prohibetur—the very idea of *law* is excluded.

on the will of a single private individual, and not on a law proceeding immediately from the supreme political power.— Under a system of caste personal liberty and the right of property are controlled by laws restraining the activity of a class of persons, more or less strictly defined, to a particular course of life, and allowing only a limited enjoyment of property and relative rights. Feudal slavery confines the person to a particular locality and a subordinate range of action. There is therein a certain degree of freedom within assigned limits, and the servitude is due rather to the state than to a single master, being the result of distinct laws more or less oppressive according to their nature and number.

§ 48. From what has been before said of positive law, in its most comprehensive sense, it appears that its existence in any one country, or nation, may be referred in its *origin* either to the legislation of some one possessor of sovereign power, (*positive* law, in the restricted sense,) or to the judicial recognition of principles founded in natural reason; while its *authority* in any particular territory, and at any particular time, depends upon its being then and there supported by some one such possessor of sovereignty, whose existence and authority is independent of *law* in the ordinary sense. And, since, in the present condition of the world, being entirely occupied by nationalities of some sort, the actual extent of that territory over which any possessor of sovereignty shall exercise dominion results from the public international action of different states, it may be said to be *determined by* international law; though it is a fact taken in jurisprudence to be independent of the will of every other national power than that which is, within that territory, the source of the municipal (national) law, both public and private.

Or, more strictly speaking, those principles which apply to, and are said by way of analogy to be a *law* for the action or intercourse of nations, and which are public or private international law, according to the character of the persons upon whom they operate, may be taken to be divided into two portions. The first consisting of principles which are not laws in the primary sense, or not rules of action, but laws in the secondary sense only,—the statements of the mode of existence or of action of states, or political bodies: which must essentially be acknowledged in every national jurisdiction as axiomatic and basal principles: (and which, therefore, enter also into municipal law.) The second portion consisting in rules of action, laws in the primary sense, which do not necessarily have the same universal recognition and extent; but which, if received by any states, or nations, regulate the reciprocal action of those states, or nations, and of the individuals of whom they are constituted, supposing such reciprocal action to take place. Each of these portions is public law, in reference to its effects on the relations of the state, or nation, regarded as a political unity, and private law, so far as it defines or affects the relations of private individuals.[1]

§ 49. The first of these portions of international law, (also entering into municipal law,) is expressed in the definitions of such terms as these,—a nation; a sovereign; sovereignty; jurisdiction; *forum;* national territory; domain; subjection; native subject; domicil; alien; alienage, &c.; which are terms necessarily used in the exposition both of municipal and international law. These terms are statements of the mode of existence of nations, or states, derived from the general reasoning of mankind in the social condition, independently of the legislative authority of any one of the states, nations, or political communities whose existence is defined by them. So far as these statements are constituent parts of positive law,—international, or municipal rules of action,—they belong to those principles which are judicially recognized as having the character of *universal law*, (herein also called from its universality the *law of nations*.) Although these principles are necessary axioms of all positive law, international or municipal, they are more frequently called principles of the law of nations in view of their application to the public existence of nations than in view of their origin and universal character. They form what has been frequently denominated, in reference both to their origin and application, "the natural, or necessary law of nations," and have been

---

[1] Bowyer: Univ. Pub. Law, 22. Therefore Hermogenianus, Dig. L. 5. De Just. et Jure, describes civil society, and the necessary transactions among men, as springing from *jus gentium*, by which he means natural law; or that which, in the words of Gaius, naturalis ratio inter omnes homines constituit.

classed with international rules of action in works which treat of that law of which nations are the subjects, because it is only in international relations, public or private, that they become subjects of judicial cognizance.[1]

§ 50. The second portion of international law consists in whatever rules of conduct nations may observe towards each other, or enforce between the individuals of whom they are respectively composed. This part of international law is more arbitrary, or has not that necessary existence which is ascribed to the first portion, being dependent upon the autonomic juridical action of states; it is, therefore, appropriately denominated positive, or practical international law.[2] But these international rules between nations are based, as also the municipal law of each, on the recognition of the definitions of their existence as nations: (which, by being so universally received, are judicially taken to belong to the universal principles, otherwise herein called *law of nations*.) The distinction in the use of the terms *international law*, and *law of nations*, which is to be here observed, is this:—*international law* is a law defined with reference to its jurisdiction, or application;—the *law of nations* is a law defined with reference to its origin, or historical character.[3]

§ 51. It is the first portion, then, of international law to which the existence, authority, and domain of any one state, or nation, is to be attributed in a legal point of view, and not those rules of action which are here called the second portion. Because, in the theory of jurisprudence at least, the existence and power of each nation is taken to be independent of those rules; or the rules themselves are a consequence of that existence, authority, and domain.

The laws, or rules of action for private persons, which are to prevail under the jurisdiction, when thus determined, of any state, or nation, are ascribed to the authority of the state as a politi-

---

[1] Reddie: Inq. in International Law, 2d ed., pp. 119—130. Vattel: Prelim., § 8. Bowyer: Univ. Pub. Law, pp. 11, 12. Some writers may, however, have employed it to signify natural equity applied to the international relations of states. See 2 Browne, Civ. and Adm. Law, p. 13–15.

[2] By Von Martens: "Positives oder pracktisches Völkerrecht." Compare an enumeration of the various synonyms used by different authors to designate these two parts of international law in Amer. Jurist, vol. xx.; article by M. Victor Foucher.

[3] Reddie: Inq. in International Law, 2d. ed., p. 410.

cal person, or to the possessor of that sovereign power in which the state consists, whether they are applied as municipal (national) or international private law; or, in other words, whether they are applied with or without reference to the existence, or juridical action of other states, or nations.[1] These laws are the *proper*, or peculiar law of that state; and in being confined to its limits and jurisdiction are known as the local, or territorial, or national law; or, what has been termed the "municipal law" in English and American jurisprudence, at least since the time of Blackstone.

§ 52. An exposition of the law prevailing within the territorial domain of any one country, or nation, is, therefore, necessarily always historical;[2] consisting in a statement of the existence of a possessor of sovereign national power, and of the exercise of that power in promulgating rules of action for private persons, either by positive legislation, or by judicial action, under its authority; and the law is necessarily described both as public and private law.

§ 53. Whatever rules of action are enforced within the domain of any one state, or nation, as its local, territorial, or national law, may apply to persons within that jurisdiction, according to any distinctions which the supreme power of that state might recognize among them; that is, the local law, by being applied to different persons according to those distinctions, becomes distinguished into different personal laws.[3] These distinctions may arise from principles which are connected with

---

[1] Bowyer: Univ. Pub. L., p. 156. "The general principle of modern times is that the territory determines the law, and the law of the territory regulates the property and contracts of all who inhabit the country. In this respect citizens differ little from foreigners, and national origin has no influence. (Savigny: Hist. R. L., French Tr., vol. i., p. 89.) We denote this state of things by the common expression, *the law of the land,* meaning the territorial law."

[2] Whewell: Elem. Morality, &c., B. ii., ch. vi., 209, 215. Reddie's Inquiries Element, &c., 24, 25. Hegel: Grundlinien der Philos. des Rechts, § 212. Tr.: "The science of positive law is to a certain extent an historical science, which has its beginning in authority, (or which begins by recognizing authority.')"

Mackeldey's Compend., § 3. "*Positive law* is the law established by historical facts, or the sum of those principles which are acknowledged in a state as principles of law, and consequently have authority as such."

In the exposition, or teaching, of jurisprudence—the science of positive law—two schools are recognized—the analytical and the historical. But there is not any real antagonism between them. See Reddie's Inq. El, p. 88.

[3] Ante, § 25. Duponceau on Jurisdiction, p. 24.

the existence of states and nations, or their mutual intercourse, and which are manifested, or employed in rules having an international application. In this manner, when the international law is applied, or enforced by any state, or nation, upon persons within its jurisdiction, and becomes identified in *authority* with the municipal (national) law thereof, it is at the same time distinguished as a personal law.[1]

In view of this difference of application, the private law prevailing within any national jurisdiction may be distinguished into municipal private law, (which, with propriety, may be called *internal*[2] private law,) and international private law, according to the character of the persons to whom it applies.

§ 54. To illustrate more fully this distinction in the application of the local, or territorial law of any one state to persons:—It is an axiomatic principle of universal law, included in that "natural and necessary law of nations," which was described as forming the first portion of international law, under the division herein before given, that the effect of sovereign power upon the legal relations of the person is co-existent with the presence of such person within the limits which the public law (international and municipal) assigns to the jurisdiction of the state, or sovereign. This actual presence, and the relation of subjection which is incurred by it, may commence either by the birth of the person, or by his entry from some foreign jurisdiction.

---

[1] Reddie's Inq. in Internat. Law, pp. 463–6. International, as well as municipal law, must also apply to things as well as persons; that is, the rights (with their correspondent obligations) which are determined by international law may be rights in respect to things; but whenever rights, or obligations, in respect to things, are ascribed to international law, as contrasted with municipal (internal) law, the law has a personal extent from the character of the persons who sustain the relations constituted by those rights and obligations.

[2] The law prevailing locally thus becomes distinguished into *internal* and *international* according to Bentham's terminology. Or it might be said to be distinguished as acting internally or internationally, according to "the *political quality* of the persons whose conduct is the object of the law. These may on any given occasion be distinguished as members of the same state, or as members of different states; in the first case, the law may be referred to the head of *internal*, in the second to the head of *international* jurisprudence." Bentham: Morals and Legislation, ch. xix., § 2, (xxv.)

Bowyer's Commentaries on Modern Civil Law, Lond., 1848, p. 18. "Thus jurists of modern times have divided public law into *internal* and *external*. The former is that which regulates the constitution and government of each community, or commonwealth, within itself, and the latter is that which concerns the intercourse of different commonwealths with each other: this is properly known by the name of *international law*."

Thus, there is a natural possibility that the same person may, at different times, be subject to different jurisdictions; and there is in every state a natural and necessary distinction between native-born subjects and alien-born subjects; which, so far, is a necessary, or axiomatic principle. But the different legal relations which make the *legal* distinction between native and alien subjects, or between temporary subjects and domiciled subjects, depend upon some rule of action enforced by the state.

The fact of being present within a particular jurisdiction, with or without concomitant circumstances, might be taken, irrespectively of the circumstances of native, or foreign birth, to be that which should determine the operation of the laws of a state upon persons within its territorial jurisdiction: in which case, the recognition of such fact becomes an axiomatic principle, in determining the relations of persons thus distinguished. A residence, or continuance, under certain conditions, to which it is not necessary here to allude more particularly, is, under the name of *domicil*, actually thus recognized: that is, it is actually taken to have a certain effect in determining the operation of the local law. The local, or territorial law of any one state or country might possibly make no distinction, between persons subject to its authority, in respect either to the circumstance of native or alien birth, or to that state of circumstances which is known as domicil: and if it were possible that there should be no recognition of legal rights and obligations arising out of relations caused by previous subjection to another dominion, there would, in that case, be no manifestation of international law, operating as private law.[1] When the local or municipal law is spoken of as applying territorially, without reference to persons as alien and native, or alien and domiciled, it is contrasted with international law—taken in the sense of a rule of which states are the subjects.

But when the rights and duties of private persons within any national dominion differ according to the circumstance of domicil or alienage; or vary as they may or may not have been subject to a foreign jurisdiction, the local or national law

---

[1] Bowyer: Univ. Pub. Law, 151-3.

is spoken of as applying differently to the persons so distinguished: and in acquiring the character of a personal law, (in contrast with a territorial law,) may be itself divided into strictly municipal, (or internal), private law, and international private law; though each part rests on the same political authority: and the condition of private persons, whether regarded as the subjects of rights and duties, or as only objects of action, (ante, § 21), is a necessary topic of one or the other of these divisions of the local, municipal, civil, or national law of each country.[1]

§ 55. According to what has been before said, every law determining the relations of natural persons, whether alien or native, is to be ascertained either from positive legislation, or by judicial recognition of laws founded in natural reason, and identified with the will of the state, (§ 29.) The autonomous decree (*esto*) of a sovereign power may attribute any rights or obligations, (being restrained only by the necessary conditions of things—§ 6,) to particular persons, or may attribute them generally to all persons within the territorial jurisdiction of that sovereign source of law.[2] The tribunal, which administers law as the pre-existing will of the state, is restricted to declaring what law *is* (*videtur*), and in the personal extent which it gives to laws must be guided by certain existent criteria.

The ascertained will of the state is binding on all within its jurisdiction; though it has unequal effect upon different persons; creating different rights and obligations, in relations in which they are the subjects of rights and duties, or the objects of action. The action of men in society being different, the relations, rights and duties of all cannot be alike.

But an individual or absolute right may be ascribed by the law of a country to any number of natural persons within its domain, though it must be exercised by each, relatively to different persons and things—the objects of action.

---

[1] Mr. Reddie uses the term *internal* law as synonymous with that law which he calls the national law—Blackstone's municipal law,—and thus loses the benefit of the distinctive term *internal* to mark this division of the national (municipal) law according to its application to different persons. See Inq. Elem. &c., p. 97.

Compare Massé: Droit Commer., Tom. i., § 37, and §§ 57–60, defining *le droit civil*, including *le droit commercial*.

[2] Compare State *v.* Manuel, 4 Dev. & Batt., N. C. Rep. p. 23.

§ 56. Such a right may attach to all domiciled persons, or to all alien persons. A certain condition or *status* of natural persons, whether consisting in rights and duties of a legal person, or in a chattel condition, may, whether determined by positive legislation or by a judicial application of natural reason, be the effect of either municipal (internal), or of international law, or of both; the extent, or application to persons, of a law originating in positive legislation, depending upon that legislation only; and there being no necessity for supposing that the dictates of natural reason on this point will be the same, in rules of action applying to alien persons, as in those relating to the native or domiciled inhabitants of any supposed national jurisdiction.

§ 57. Or the state, or supreme power, may attribute any individual right or rights to each natural person within its domain, whether domiciled or alien. In this case, the law attributing those rights, would, in the jurisprudence of that state, be a *universal* principle in respect to its *personal extent;* that is, in applying equally to each natural person. In this case, the *individual* rights so attributed are not only distinguishable from *relative* rights by existing in respect to the whole community, independently of relations towards specific persons and things, (ante, § 40,) but they may be called *absolute*, or *primordial*, or *natural* rights, because the law attributes them to natural persons simply as such, or as beings possessing the human form and nature, and as an intrinsic element of their human character.

§ 58. The extent of any principle or rule affecting the *status* of private persons is always subject to the supreme legislative power. But in the absence of such legislation, it must be determined by judicial criteria of natural reason as before set forth. (§§ 29 to 36.) Rules or principles determining the condition or *status* of natural persons may be derived from universal jurisprudence. But it is to be borne in mind, that, in being so derived into the jurisprudence of any one state, they do not, therefore, have the universal *personal extent* which is above spoken of. This *extent* of a personal law being dependent upon the will of the state in which it is applied; while a universal *character*, ascribed to any principle, has reference to its juridical source or origin; that is, depends upon the fact of its having been applied by *all nations*, or the greater part, (ante, §§ 36—38:) which application may have been in respect to a greater or less proportion of persons.

The different extent of laws to natural persons according to their subjection at different times to different national jurisdictions, and the mode in which, by the application of international law to the relations of private persons, universal jurisprudence may be distinctly recognized, and local or territorial laws, affecting condition or *status*, may receive universal personal extent, will be considered in the following chapter.

NOTE.—The following extract from an Essay by Henry Sumner Maine, LL. D., On the Conception of Sovereignty, and its importance in International Law—Papers read before the Juridical Society, London, June, 1855—p. 26, may, with some readers, serve to justify expressions in the text, which may at first appear to be an attempt after a useless novelty of expression. Speaking of Austin's Province of Jurisprudence Determined, Dr. Maine says, p. 29: "And here, as I have alluded to Mr. Austin's treatise, I trust I may be pardoned for saying that I know no reason, *but one*, why it has not long since dispelled the indifference to the systematic study of Jurisprudence which was so eloquently lamented at the inaugural meeting of this society. [By Sir Richard Bethell, p. 1, of the same tract.] The one drawback on its usefulness has been its *style*—which is such as to repel a superficial reader, and not to attract even a patient one; but it would be foolish not to admit that there are abundant excuses for the peculiarity. England has no literature of jurisprudence; consequently, the English language comprises no true juristical phraseology. Our English law terms are strictly terms of art, and it would be absurd to attempt to strain them beyond their well-defined, long accepted, and technical meaning. The language, then, which must be used for questions of universal jurisprudence is popular language, infected with all the vices of common speech, vague, figurative and general. In employing it for such an examination of these questions as is appropriate to closet study, it is necessary to be constantly limiting and qualifying it, to be perpetually weeding it of metaphor, and to be carefully cleaning it from the misleading suggestions which lurk in mere arrangements of words and collocations of phrase. Among the numberless advantages which may be looked for from an extended study of Roman law, I am not sure that the highest will not be the introduction of a terminology, neither too rigid for employment upon points of the philosophy of law, nor too lax and elastic for their lucid and accurate discussion."

CHAPTER II.

FARTHER CONSIDERATION OF THE NATURE OF PRIVATE INTERNATIONAL LAW: ITS ORIGIN AND APPLICATION. ITS EFFECT UPON CONDITIONS OF FREEDOM AND BONDAGE.

§ 59. In the definition of international law which was given in the first chapter, it was shown to have the name of *a law* only by an improper use of the term, when considered as a rule of action for states in their several entity or personality; since, though it consists of a recognized body of rules distinct from the municipal (national) law of each state or nation, it is not prescribed to them by a superior, but operates upon them as political persons, or upon private persons within their respective domain, only by their own several allowance or consent. This being the legal or juridical view of the obligation of that law; whatever may be its source in a divine rule of action, or law of nature. When, therefore, private international law operates upon private persons, in any national jurisdiction, by the allowance of the supreme power of the state, it has, in respect to such persons, the same sanction and force as the municipal (national) law, and, as to all persons who are distinct from the state or sovereign, it has equally the effect and authority of *law* in the proper meaning of the term. The distinction of private international law from private municipal (internal) law arising, not from a difference in the nature of their authority over individuals, but in the character of the relations which they severally affect.

§ 60. When considering, in the first chapter, the mode in which positive law becomes known as the law of some one state or country (§ 48), the international law was described as being divided into two portions. The first consisting of laws in the *secondary* sense only,—necessary axioms, or definitions of the political existence of states,—entering into both international and municipal (national) law. The second, consisting of laws in the *primary* sense—rules of action—which may, or may not, exist, or be observed, between specified states. The first portion, which, as was remarked in the same place, corresponds with that which is sometimes called "the natural, or necessary law of nations," but which indicates at the same time relations of private persons, as well as the relations of states. may indeed be taken to be antecedent to, and independent of, the power of any one state: but the rules of action which compose the second portion, whatever authority they may have in natural reason, become *law* for private individuals only by being enforced by the power which promulgates the municipal (national) law of that jurisdiction or state in which the person may be found.

§ 61. If, then, it is asked—wherein does private international law consist, as a rule of action in any one national jurisdiction, distinct from the municipal (internal) law of that jurisdiction? —the answer must be found by ascertaining the effect of the necessary axiomatic principles or definitions composing the first part of the international law, as before described, upon private persons and upon things; and next—the actual allowance or creation of rights and obligations of private persons, as the incidents of legal relations which have an international character from the fact that the agents and objects of action presupposed in them are persons, or persons and things, not altogether or exclusively under the juridical power of a single nation or state: those persons, or those persons and things being discriminated, by the application of the axiomatic principles above spoken of, as persons subject to different jurisdictions; such persons being alien, or native, domiciled, or temporary subjects in reference to some one jurisdiction or *forum*.

§ 62. The terms or phrases by which the nature or mode of existence of states or nations is set forth or defined, are so generally known in the maxims of public law, that it is not necessary here to attempt any separate exposition of them: though it may become necessary hereafter to consider particularly the meaning of some of those terms, as they may be used in stating international or municipal (internal) rules of action.

The general principles or maxims which are contained in the definition of these terms, are set forth most at large by writers who treat of public international law, regarded as a rule of imperfect obligation (*ante*, § 11,) of which states or nations are the subjects; though they are equally presupposed in rules determining the relations of private persons towards those states or nations, and having the force of law in the strict sense—i. e., public municipal (national) law.

§ 63. Upon an examination of these maxims, as stated by writers on public law, it will be seen that there are *three* which may be taken for the most general or fundamental; and which are in fact but one and the same definition of sovereignty;—or they are assertions, in different forms, of the essential character of sovereignty; or, again,—descriptions of sovereign national power in three different relations. The first being a definition of sovereign national power considered, as it may be said, absolutely,—or in relation to its own materials, or constituent parts; without reference to the existence of any other manifestation or embodiment of that kind of power: which may be thus stated:—

I. *The power of every state, or nation, is absolute, self-dependent, or supreme, within that space, or territory, which it possesses, or occupies, as its own domain, and over all persons and things therein.*

The second maxim is but the same assertion expressed relatively to the co-existence of several states, or nations; recognizing the limitation of each by the fact of the equally independent existence of the others; this is, that—

II. *The sovereign power of one state, or nation, is not to be recognized as sovereign, or has no existence, as such, beyond its own domain, or territory, or within the space, or territory, which constitutes the domain of another possessor of national sovereignty.*

§ 64. These two maxims, when taken for maxims of international law, belong to the first portion of international law, according to the division herein before made, (*ante*, § 48,) since they can be called *laws* in the secondary sense only; not being properly rules of action, but statements of a mode of existence, or of action. They must lie at the foundation of all positive law; and they have in jurisprudence the character, or extent of *universal law*—the *law of nations*, (*jus gentium*,) because actually asserted, or proclaimed, and universally received, by nations, or states, as being natural and necessary principles.[1]

In the manifestation of this sovereign power, over persons and things, by states, or nations, originates *law* in the primary sense—rules of action; forming relations between persons in respect to other persons, and in respect to things. Since these relations are legal,—that is, are known as the effects of law, it is a consequence of the two maxims just stated, that they have existence only in some one jurisdiction in which that law is known as a coercive rule proceeding from the sovereign of such jurisdiction, and the rights and obligations composing those relations have no legal force beyond it.

§ 65. It was remarked in the first chapter that international law (public and private) arises from the necessarily existing circumstance that the whole variety of human interests and action cannot, from their nature, (or, it may be said, from their relation to space and time,) be distinctly divided among, and separately included under the limits of single states; and yet the juridical power of society must be supposed, in some form, either by enjoining, permitting, or prohibiting, to be exerted upon interests and actions which are not so included under the exclusive dominion of single states, (*ante*, § 10.) The effect of law is exhibited in legal relations, comprehending rights, with their corresponding obligations, in respect to persons, and in respect to things. The action involved in any legal relation must take place in reference both to space and time; and the conceivability of relations whose legal existence is indeterminable under the law of a single state, (which conception supposes an international law according to the definition in the first chapter,) will arise from postulates of their existence in respect to space and in respect to time: such relations being, also, dis-

[1] Bowyer: Univer. Public Law, p. 151, and the citations.

tinguishable among themselves by differences in the comparative effect of space and time in connecting their legal existence with the juridical action of more than one state.

For, *first*, relations may be supposed, or conceived, not to be exclusively determinable by the juridical power of a single state, by reason of differences in the respective geographical positions, at one and the same time, of the persons and things which are to be the subjects and objects of the rights therein involved.[1]

And, *secondly*, other relations may be supposed, or conceived, not to be so determinable under the juridical power of a single state, by reason of differences in the respective times at which the persons, or the persons and things, which are to be the subjects and objects of the rights involved in those relations are together found within different geographical jurisdictions: they being at one time within the territorial dominion of one state, and afterwards within that of another.

§ 66. It will be seen in comparing these classes of relations that there is a manifest difference in the degree in which it may be said that they are *not* exclusively determinable under the juridical power (the law) of single states.

In the class of relations first described, the persons and things which are to be the subjects and objects of the rights involved in those relations, not being at the same time under the same jurisdiction, it is actually impossible, from the axiomatic principles of jurisprudence, (natural and necessary law of nations,) that the action in which those rights must be manifested should take place without a concurrent juridical action on the part of the respective states, either producing one common rule, or consenting to the controlling operation of rules proceeding from one or from the other. In this case it may be said that the question—by which juridical power the relation is to be determined?—precedes the legal existence of the relation.

[1] Wheaton : International Law, Part ii., ch. 2. "It often happens that an individual possesses real property in a state other than that of his domicile, or that contracts are entered into and testaments executed by him in a country different from either, or that he is interested in successions *ab intestato* in such third country ; it may happen that he is at the same time subject to two or three sovereign powers—to that of his native country, or of his domicile, or to that of the place where the property in question is situated, and to that of the place where the contracts have been made, or the acts executed."

But, in the other class of relations, the persons and things which are to be the subjects and objects of the rights involved in those relations, having been together under the juridical power of one state before the other is supposed to have any possible operation, the existence of a relation between them precedes the question—by which juridical power the legal force of that relation is to be determined?—: and there is not any actual impossibility that the action in which those rights must be manifested should take place without a concurrent juridical action on the part of the respective states; the persons and things between whom the relation is supposed to exist, being, at different times, under the exclusive dominion of some one juridical power.

§ 67. Now from the possible connexion, in respect to persons and things, which is here indicated between distinct sources of law having separate jurisdictions, arises the third of the three fundamental maxims before enumerated; which, like the two already stated, is only a recognition of sovereign states or nations as being the independent sources of positive law, even while stating this possible relation or connexion between them; which maxim may be thus expressed:—

III. *The laws of one nation or state may, by the consent or allowance, and therefore under the authority of the supreme national power in another nation or state, have the effect of law within the jurisdiction of the latter.*

This maxim, it will at once be perceived, is from the meaning of the term *law*, inconsistent, except as it is merely another form of the first and second. For the law—being a rule of action resting on the authority of some one sovereign—if the laws of one state can be said to take effect in the jurisdiction of another, they are in fact the law of the state in which they take effect, and not of the first.[1]

---

[1] Compare Story's Confl. L., § 21, 22. Fœlix Droit International Privé, § 10, 11. Schæffner in Entwicklung des Internat. Privatrechts, § 26, cites Zachariä, as saying. (Tr.) "Each right, and in the same degree each obligation, subsists exclusively under the laws of the land in which the right or the obligation (according to the effect of those laws) is to be enforced and is enforced under the supposed circumstances. This rule, (which in fact is merely a reiteration of the well known maxim, *Leges non valent extra territorium,* in the only sense which can be given to it,) is derived, immediately, from the sovereignty of states. For if it should be held that the law of a particular

PLACE OF THE THIRD MAXIM.

§ 68. The first two of these three maxims are necessary propositions in defining what sovereign national power is; and lie at the foundation of all positive law—municipal (internal) or international. The third is not *necessary* in the same sense: being the statement of a manifestation of sovereign power which may or may not take place. It is however the statement of a relation or condition only; and therefore, like the first and second, a law in the secondary sense of the word *law*. It is an axiom of public law lying at the foundation of that which is herein before called *private* international law;—so far as such international law can be judicially recognized in any national jurisdiction, as distinct from the private municipal (internal) law of that jurisdiction:—private *international* law;—which, as described in the first chapter, determines the *realization* of the legal relations of private persons in those interests and actions which cannot subsist or have not continued under the exclusive territorial authority of any one state or nationality: (§ 10) which relations, with the rights and obligations of which they are composed, must yet, primarily at least, as is implied in these three maxims, receive their legal *existence* under some one municipal (national) law.[1]

---

state may, or must, as such, be carried into effect in another state, the legislative power of the former state could be extended over the latter, and in proportion diminish its legislative power;—the chief attribute of sovereignty. It is true that the application and execution of the foreign law would always remain with the judicial and administrative officers of the forum.. But the rule according to which these officers would decide and act would have been prescribed by a foreign government. And how can they be empowered to act according to this rule, when they are only the instruments or servants of the government by which they were appointed." To this proposition the same author states three cases of exceptions, allowing them to be such in appearance only. Schæffner calls the proposition a novel one, and denies its correctness. There is probably no real contrariety of opinion between them. Apparently Zachariä, in discriminating the law to which he should attribute the relation, looks to the political authority which coercively maintains the rights and obligations in which it consists, and therefore speaks of it as subsisting under the law of the forum; while the other looks to the legislator whose moral judgment attributed those rights and obligations to the persons between whom the relation is maintained, and therefore regards the relation as possibly subsisting under the law of a foreign state.

[1] The *realization*—the actualization—the carrying-out of. The term employed for this by some German writers of reputation is—the *Verwirklichung*—the making or the being made *wirklich*—real or actual. Another term nearly equivalent is the *Geltendmachen*—the making *geltend*—available, or in force. And this is distinguished from the *Existent-werden*—the becoming, or the being made existent. Thus it is said by Schæffner § 27. " A very different thing from the *Existent-werden*, (the being made, or the becoming existent,) is the *Geltend-machen* (the putting in force, or the being made available,) that is, the assertion that a certain fact (legal effect) has become *verwirk-*

§ 69. The municipal (national) law of any one state may contain rules of action applying originally, and as a law of local origin, to the relations of private persons within its jurisdiction, who are distinguished by the supreme power as alien, which are not rules that take notice of the effects of the laws of foreign jurisdictions in creating rights and obligations for those persons. Rules of this kind can be called international (as contrasted with internal) only in being founded on the simple distinction between native and alien subjects.[1] The private international law then, so far as it can be distinguished from the municipal (internal) law of any one jurisdiction, is, in its form and manifestation, a rule regulating in that jurisdiction the admission or allowance of different municipal (internal) laws, or of their effects; being properly called *private*, because determining rights and obligations arising out of relations of private persons: whether the municipal (internal) law, first establishing these relations, is principally of a national and public character, or is more strictly private.

§ 70. The three maxims or propositions above given can in their nature be only statements of the self-existent or self-dependent nature of nations, states, or sovereignties, and therefore *laws* in the secondary sense of the word only. If the attempt is made to go beyond these, and state a rule under which this international recognition of municipal (national) laws, (the possibility of which only is implied or stated in the third maxim,) should take effect, or will take effect—a law having the force of a rule of action—a law in the primary sense, it is evident that such rule may be stated either in the form of a rule of which states or nations are the subjects, determining their respective rights and obligations, or, in the form of a rule of which private persons are the subjects. In the first alternative, the rule can only be law in the imperfect sense, or a law of the imperfect kind, and cannot determine the action of such states or nations except

---

licht (realized—actualized—carried out,) under the jurisdiction of a certain law." But Waechter in his treatise (published in the same year, 1841,) on the collision of laws in Archiv. f. d. Civil. Praxis, vol. 24, p. 237, takes the word *verwirklicht*, as employed in a citation from Struve, in a sense which appears to be directly opposite to that above given. The first necessity in questions of this kind is a received nomenclature.

[1] Such as naturalization laws, police laws relating to immigrants.

by being identified with their several autonomic will or consent; and it will be *public* international law, from the character of the persons upon whom it operates, or for whom it is said to be a rule. In the second alternative the rule may have the coercive character of positive law, in reference to the action of private persons, and be a rule which judicial tribunals may apply, or will be bound to apply in determining the rights and obligations of such persons, in relations in respect to other persons and in respect to things; being *private* international law from the character of the persons upon whom it operates, or for whom it is said to be a rule. But it is evident with regard to the possibility of any such rule—a rule having the character of positive law,—that it must be part of some municipal (national) law; that is, it must, according to previous definition, be identified with, or rather must derive its existence from, the ascertained will of some legislator,—some political person vested with the authority of society or of the state.

Now to whatever degree the state or nation, or the possessors of supreme or sovereign power, may, in their political entity or personality, be bound (by public international law—the law of "positive morality"—*Austin, ante* § 11, n.) to allow foreign laws to take effect within their own jurisdiction, their judicial tribunals have the like duty, in allowing or refusing the international admission of foreign laws, which they have in enforcing the municipal law strictly so called—the internal law—the law operating within each national jurisdiction irrespectively of the existence of other such jurisdictions; they must ascertain the will of the supreme power of the state in reference to such international allowance.

§ 71. It will be remembered that the relations which it was supposed might be indeterminable under the legislative power, or the law of a single state were herein before divided or classified by differences in the comparative effect of space and time in connecting their legal existence with the legislative action of more than one state, (*ante* § 65.)

In regard to the first class of relations—that namely in which the persons and things, which are to be the subjects and objects of the rights involved in those relations, are not all supposed to be at one time under one and the same jurisdiction, (in which case the question, by which legislative power the relation is to be determined, would precede the existence of the relation, and where it would be impossible that the action in which those rights must be manifested should take place without some concurrent legislative action on the part of the respective states within which those persons and things should be found, either producing one common rule or consenting to the controlling operation of rules proceeding from one or from the other,)—the question of the existence and determination of these relations, when raised before a *judicial tribunal*, may appropriately receive the name of a question of *the conflict of laws;* which name has been given by Huber, Story, and others, to cases determined by private international law as herein described.

That name, however, is evidently less appropriate to express the question of the existence and determination of the second class of relations, before described: since, according to the supposition, the persons between whom they are to exist, or the persons and things who are to be the subjects and objects of the right involved in that relation, are always at some one time under the exclusive dominion of some one state.

§ 72. The international determination of the first class of relations constitutes one of those topics of jurisprudence wherein it has been found most difficult for judicial tribunals, or for private jurists and law writers, to agree in *a priori* deductions from elementary and necessary principles.[1] Rules, however, may exist, in regard to this class of relations, in the jurisprudence of any one country, either originating in positive legislation or in judicial precedent, which, of course, must be taken to have been intended for jural rules, or rules founded in natural reason, and not merely arbitrary and accidental determinations. And so far as any rules are found to have been concurrently adopted in the jurisprudence of different nations, they thereby acquire the character of a universal jurisprudence or *law of nations;* and there is in that fact an authority for the judicial tribunals of any

---

[1] To these rules the citation given by Schæffner, § 22, note, well applies:—" Leyser; Med. ad Pand. Sp. 283, p. 1162. says in regard to Farinacius and others. Regulas in is multas inveni, sed quando eas cum subjectis limitationibus contuli, ipsarum regularum nihil superesse vidi."

one country or state, (in the silence of the local legislation or customary law on that point,) to adopt them, as being presumptively accordant with the legislative will of the nation or state whose juridical authority they exercise.[1] But it appears to have been difficult, even by such an *a posteriori* or inductive method, to discover any harmonious and consistent system of rules applicable in such cases.[2]

The determination of the second class of relations is simpler, because the relations are first taken to be *in existence* under the legislative action of one state or nation, or one possessor of sovereign power, and the question is of their *continuance* or *realization* under the legislative and juridical power of another.

§ 73. Since *status* or personal condition, as defined in the first chapter, consists principally in the possession of individual rights, and the relations of which it is an incident do not imply the exercise of rights relative to specific things, it must always be at any one time under the legislative power of some one state; that is, the state within whose actual territorial jurisdiction the natural person may be found, whose *status* or personal condition is to be determined. So far, therefore, as it may become a topic of private international law, it appears as an incident of the relations of the second class above described. That is to say, the *status* of a natural person can become a question of private international law, only when such person is supposed to have had a *status* or personal condition in relations created under some foreign law, which relations being regarded as existing or having existed under the foreign law—the question is of their *realization*, *actualization*, or continuance.

Since the inquiries to be pursued in the following pages will be limited to questions connected with the law of *status* or condition, private international law will in this chapter be further considered only as it may determine relations of the second of the two classes above described.

---

[1] The principle—*locus regit actum,* when applied to this class of cases, may however be cited as an example. And compare Savigny: Heut. R. R., B. 3, c. i, § 348. The eighth volume of this work of Savigny relates exclusively to the conflict of laws.

[2] Saul *vs.* His Creditors, 17, Martin's Rep. Louisiana, 569, by the court: "We know of no matter in jurisprudence so unsettled, or none, that should more teach men distrust of their own opinions, and charity for those of others."

§ 74. Although the question before the tribunal determining the *status*, or condition of private persons under international law, regards the maintenance of legal relations of persons, or of correlative rights and duties of persons, in respect to persons and things included under a certain national jurisdiction, those relations, or those rights and obligations, are not, by the very implication of the third maxim, to be regarded as entirely dependent, or not so in the first instance, upon that municipal (internal) law which is the territorial law, or local law, of that jurisdiction in which those persons and things are found. Whenever a question is made of the determination, under private international law, of rights and duties incident to the class of relations now under consideration, a recognition of private persons as aliens, in respect either of birth or of domicil, or at least as having been anteriorly subject to some other jurisdiction, is pre-supposed; and the private international law (i. e., that part of the national law of the jurisdiction which is to determine that question,) is applied as a *personal* law,—a law attaching to certain persons in virtue of their anterior subjection to a foreign jurisdiction, irrespective of the general territorial operation of that municipal (internal) law of the *forum* to which they are, or have been, alien in a greater or less degree, or under a greater or less variety of circumstances, (*ante*, § 53.)

It was stated in the first chapter, that the contrasted relations (conditions) of alien and native subjects are necessary or axiomatic ideas in international law, being stated in those definitions which form the first portion of international law (public and private) according to the division there given. But the fact of mere subjection, independently of place of birth, to different jurisdictions, is that upon which the distinction of an international law—being a rule determining the relations of private persons, and operating as part of the municipal (national) law of some one state, or nation—is founded. It being possible that within the jurisdiction of any particular state persons may be present who have been subject to the territorial jurisdiction of another, the laws of the first may be conceived of as making no distinction between them and others in consequence of that fact. But the laws of a state are not necessarily nor usually thus equally operative. All within a national jurisdiction are equally subject to the supreme power of the state, but the laws therein (i. e., the national law,) may apply differently to natives, and to those originally coming from another national jurisdiction. This difference in the application of the national law may be combined with the recognition of the rights and obligations of private persons in relations caused by a foreign law to which they have been previously subject; and there may be a difference in the degree of this recognition, and in the extent of the local, or territorial law of the *forum* to persons who are not native, by discriminating between them in respect to their being either permanent and domiciled, or transient and temporary subjects. When the previous actual, or territorial subjection of certain private persons to a foreign law is judicially recognized in the *forum* of jurisdiction, and the question is made of the realization or continuance therein of rights and obligations of those persons in relations existing under that foreign law, then the local or national law operates as private international law. For though this distinction between persons is made under some municipal (national) law—i. e., some law known as the positive law of some one nation, or state—that law, being differently applied to persons thus discriminated, or distinguished,—may be denominated *international*, because it then determines the operation of the municipal (national) laws of different countries, or states. In these cases, the relations of certain persons are recognized simply *as facts* existing by the operation of a foreign law; but the validity of the rights and obligations included in them is determined solely by the local juridical authority. And so far as the tribunals of the *forum* are concerned, the relations existing under the foreign law are to be brought to their judicial cognizance by proof, like other facts: they are not legal effects which the tribunal is bound independently to take notice of.[1]

§ 75. When persons and things pass from one national jurisdiction into another, it is impossible, in the nature of things, that all the relations in which they were the subjects, or objects of rights and duties under the law of their original jurisdiction,

[1] Fœlix: Dr. Int. Pr., § 18. Story: Conf. L., § 637, and the cases cited.

should exist under the jurisdiction to which they have been removed; because all the persons and things which were with them the subjects, or objects of corresponding rights, or duties, in those relations, are not transferred with them to the new jurisdiction. It is not, therefore, supposable, when persons thus pass from one jurisdiction into another, that all their rights and obligations, existing under the law of the first jurisdiction, should be maintained by the law of the second. That class of rights of persons, which in the first chapter were called *absolute*, or *individual* rights, may (since they exist in a relation of individual persons to the whole community, without distinction of specific individuals in it, and as rights of action have no determinate, or special objects,) continue to be, for the subjects of them, the same in effect; though the objects may be different, and the supreme power sustaining them is a different political personality. But those rights (the right *to* private property, or *of* private property, for instance,) so far as they are relative to specific persons and things, and those rights which were in the same chapter called *relative*, because arising under relations of persons to other determinate persons, cannot, it is plain, subsist under the law of the new jurisdiction unless the persons and things which are the relative subjects and objects of those rights are transferred to the new jurisdiction. But it is plain that so far as the action implied in any legal relation continues to be physically possible, notwithstanding a change of place on the part of the persons between whom, or the persons and things in respect to whom, or to which that relation has once subsisted, any of the rights of persons arising out of a relation constituted by the law of one jurisdiction, may be allowed to retain the character of a legal right, under the sovereign authority of the new jurisdiction. Whenever this is the case, the supreme national authority, having independent power in a specified territory, adopts the law of another, or allows it to take effect therein as a law of foreign origin; though its authority as *law*, in the strict sense, must always in that jurisdiction depend on the local sovereignty.

§ 76. Since, then, this allowance, or disallowance, depends on the same authority as the municipal (internal) law, it must be ascertained in the same manner as the municipal (internal) law, resting on that authority, is ascertained. According to the view given in the first chapter of the manner in which the will of the supreme authority in states becomes expressed or assumes the form of law, that will may be ascertained either—1; from the direct expression of the will of the state in positive legislation, (*esto;*) or, 2; from an interpretation of natural reason by tribunals appointed by the state, (*videtur.*) If the sovereign or supreme power has expressed its will by legislative enactment or action having that effect, that expression is equally authoritative and controlling in this case as in the case of relations falling under municipal law strictly so called, (the internal law.) If no such expression exists, the tribunal must make this allowance or disallowance by reverting to the law of natural reason, as it reverts to the same for the presumed legislative will of the sovereign in enforcing the municipal or internal law. And, however autonomic or independent in its estimate of natural reason, as bearing on the relations of nations to each other, or of its own obligations (under that international law, which, as a law binding on states, is a law in the imperfect sense only,) the possessor of supreme legislative power, or the national sovereignty of any state may be when allowing or repudiating the effects of foreign laws, the judicial tribunals of any nation, at the present day, in pronouncing a judgment upon the same point, can refer only, either, as has just been said, to the positive legislation of the sovereign, or to standards of natural reason which have, by anterior judicial recognition and the implied sanction of the sovereign power whose will they execute, acquired the authority of law. These are—judgments of antecedent tribunals under the same national authority in like international cases; customs which have existed under that authority; accepted expositions of law by private persons; and, in cases where these domestic precedents do not furnish a criterion applicable to the case in question, the laws, usages, and judgments of other nations, *in respect to the international* recognition of the laws of foreign states, may be referred to, on the same principle by which such tribunals refer to the municipal (national) laws of other nations for an exposition of natural reason to be applied as their own local or municipal (internal) law—the principle, namely, that, from the nature of society and of states, the laws of all states are to be taken to intend to conform to natural right, or are promulgated for jural rules, and may be judicially referred to, by the tribunals of any one nation, as an exposition of natural reason to guide in the administration of its own (national) law—whether internal or international law—in cases where the other standards of the will of the state which are more direct, do not give a sufficient rule. The limits of an autonomous judgment on the part of a judicial tribunal being, at the present day, extremely narrow.

§ 77. The propriety of this reference by the courts of any one nation, is, as to such courts in nations wherein laws have long been administered, based upon precedent—the usage of their predecessors.[1] But the principle upon which such reference is made becomes itself, when once established, a rule of particular force in the international recognition of relations which have been created by foreign law; or—to employ a different form of expression—becomes more directly operative as a principle of the international private law. For, since the tribunal, in the case supposed, is necessarily proceeding on the supposition that the state, where it has not declared its will by positive legislation, must still be presumed to will that which is accordant with natural reason, it would follow—from the very nature of the assumption, which is above stated, in favor of the jural character of foreign laws,—that the state will recognize and support foreign laws and their effects upon persons and things coming within its dominion, when those laws are not contrary to the rule of right contained in the municipal (internal) law:[2] for if such a rule exists in that internal or local law, and

---

[1] Smith's Compend. Merc. Law, p. 6. "Here it should be observed, that the foreign laws and foreign lawyers, who have been just mentioned as having influenced the formation of the mercantile law of this country, were never, at any period, recognized by the judges of our courts as being *per se* of any authority whatever. Respected the rules which they laid down may be, for the learning and sagacity which they evince, but, when they are obeyed, it is part of the law and custom of England, declared to be such, either by long usage and tradition, or by the decisions of our own courts of justice, containing an enlightened adaptation of ancient principle to modern convenience," &c.

[2] Potter *vs.* Brown, 5 East, 530, by Lord Ellenborough. "We always import, together with their persons, the existing relations of foreigners as between themselves,

it is applicable to persons in circumstances of natural condition similar to those in which the persons known as aliens are found, it must control, so far as applicable, all rights and obligations of those aliens, and overrule the relations created by the foreign law,—by the very supposition on which the presumption in favor of a judicial recognition of the effect of the foreign law is based, viz. :—that the state—the legislator of the forum intends to enforce jural rules, or laws which are rules of right—*jus*.

§ 78. It is this principle arising out of the jural nature of society, or of the state, and the method in which law is judicially ascertained, which is the true basis of, and the warrant for that *judicial* recognition of rights and obligations of private persons in relations created by foreign laws,[1] which is commonly referred to the operation of the *comity* or good will of *nations*, and the prospect of reciprocal advantage. That recognition or allowance of the foreign law being then supposed to depend upon a *judicial* estimate of what comity or the prospect of reciprocal advantage requires the nation, for which the tribunal is acting juridically, to allow.

It is evident that if comity or good will, or the prospect of reciprocal advantage is, or ought to be, a motive acting on states and nations—the possessors of sovereign legislative power—and if it does, in an ethical point of view, require states or nations in their political personality to allow foreign laws to operate within their territory, or to recognize relations created by foreign laws, it is still only a part of *public* international law, from the character of the persons upon whom it operates, and a law in the imperfect sense only, or of an imperfect kind only— a part of positive morality, operating on states. And though it may be admitted that it *ought so* to operate upon any particular state, it still will be the duty of judicial tribunals to ascertain the will of the state upon that point, before allowing or giving effect to the foreign law in any case. It is further evident that when the will of such state on this point has been

according to the laws of their respective communities; except, indeed, where these laws clash with the rights of our own subjects here, and one or other of the laws must necessarily give way, in which case our own is entitled to the preference."

[1] Therefore this judicial recognition of foreign laws, or of their effects, is not derived *a priori*, or founded on an *a priori* juristical theory. See Reddie's Inq. El. &c., p. 230.

ascertained, it is entirely immaterial, in jurisprudence, the science of positive law, to inquire what may have been the motive acting on the state or nation, exercising sovereign legislative and juridical power, which induced it to allow or require this international recognition of foreign laws. The tribunal has simply to consider it as the rule of right established by the state. And it would be, for the tribunal and for private persons, equally law and a jural rule if it should have been caused by selfishness or enmity, and be reciprocally disadvantageous.

§ 79. This doctrine of an international comity being the basis of the *judicial* recognition of foreign laws and their effects appears to have originated in the third of Huber's three maxims, so often cited in works on international law. These are, (Huberi: Præl., Lib. i., Tit. 3. De Confl. L., § 2):—

1. Leges cujusque imperii vim habent, intra terminos ejusdem reipublicæ, omnesque ei subjectos obligant, nec ultra. *Per l. ult. ff. de Jurisdict.*[1]

2. Pro subjectis imperio habendi sunt omnes qui intra terminos ejusdem reperiuntur, sive in perpetuum, sive ad tempus ibi commorentur. *Per l. 7, § 10, in fin. de Interd. et Releg.*[2]

3. Rectores imperiorum id comiter agunt, ut jura cujusque populi intra terminos ejus exercita teneant ubique suam vim, quatenus nihil potestati aut juri alterius imperantis ejusque civium præjudicetur.

The third of these maxims resembles the third of the three herein before given, in being only the statement of a condition of things—a law in the secondary sense: but it differs in not stating the *possibility* of such international allowance, but the fact that it *is* actually made by the rulers of empires, rectores imperiorum; and it differs, still further, in not only stating the fact, but also the motive or reason which induces the supreme power, the rectores imperiorum, to make that allowance —that is, the motive of *comity*. But it is not here stated that judicial tribunals, which are not rectores imperiorum, may or do, *from comity*, make this admission in any case, until they have ascertained that it is the will of the sovereign power for

---

[1] This citation is the same as Dig. L. ii., Tit. i., 20.
[2] This citation is the same as Dig. L. xlviii., Tit. 22, 7, § 10, *in finem*.

whom they act judicially—the rector imperii—to make it.
When that will has been ascertained, it is immaterial what may
have been the motive operating on the supreme power or the
sovereign source of the national law. There is, therefore, in
this maxim, nothing making comity a judicial rule—or something, the extent and limits of which are to be judged of by
the judicial tribunal.

§ 80. It being, however, assumed that the actual legislative
and juridical practice of nations is one of the criteria by which
the tribunals of any one nation are to ascertain that law of natural reason which they are juridically to apply as the positive
law of the state—the fact that different nations, (or the civilized
nations of Europe and America,) have severally sanctioned this
international allowance, so far as not prejudicial to the *potestas*
and *jus* of the state, or of its citizens, may be taken to be an
authority for the tribunal[1] to make this international allowance
in matters of private law, when not contrary to the potestas
and jus of the state, or of its citizens; quatenus nihil potestati
aut juri alterius imperantis ejusque civium præjudicetur. These
words are translated by Story: Conf. of L., § 29,—"so far as
they do not prejudice the powers or rights of other governments
or of their citizens." The word *juri* here translated "*rights
of*," &c., might more correctly be translated *law*; or, better—
law and right: the word *jus* having the sense not only of *a
right* but also of *a law;* in the sense of a *rule of right*, a jural
law—that which must be judicially recognized as *right*, as well
as law.[2] But then it is evident that the tribunal has nothing to

---

[1] 1 Burge Comm., p. 5. "Hence, by that which is sometimes called the *comitas
gentium*, but which is at other times and more properly called the common necessity or
the mutual advantage of nations, *la nécessité du bien public et général des nations*, it is
established as a principle of international jurisprudence that effect should be given to
the laws of another state whenever the rights of a litigant before its tribunals are derived from, or are dependent on, those laws, and when such recognition is not prejudicial to its own interests or the rights of its own subjects."

Judge Bradford, in *Ex parte* Dawson, 3 Bradford's R., 135, having reference to the
action of an English *judicial tribunal* and its obligation to recognize the effects of the
law of the State of New York in the case, says, citing the above passage: "It may
also be safely laid down that from comity and considerations of mutual interest, foreign
states recognize and give effect almost universally to those laws of the domicil," &c.,
"respect being had in this particular to the sentence of the appropriate tribunal in the
place of domicil."

[2] The meaning of the word *jus*, in Roman jurisprudence, will be particularly examined in a succeeding chapter.

do with the *comity* or any other motive which may be supposed to have acted on those states, or which may or may not, for the future, influence the sovereign, *rector imperii*, whose judicial function it exercises. It is enough for the tribunal that such has been the practice of nations. Another statement of this axiom by Huber, in the treatise, Jus publicum Universale, Lib. 3, cap. 8, § 7, is also cited by writers on international law. "Summas potestates cujusque reipublicæ indulgere sibi mutuo, ut jura legesque aliorum in aliarum territoriis effectum habeant, quatenus sine præjudicio indulgentium fieri potest. Ob reciprocam utilitatem in disciplinam juris gentium abiit, ut civitas alterius civitatis leges apud se valere patiatur."[1]

If this maxim of Huber is intended only for a statement of the fact that this is the practice of nations, it is entirely unnecessary to allege comity or reciprocal advantage as the cause. As a principle of private law, it is sufficient to say that the admission has been so generally made that it has become a principle of *universal jurisprudence*, which the tribunals of every nation are bound, in the absence of a particular national rule— statutory or customary—to receive as a rule of natural reason accepted by the state. And this, perhaps, was the meaning of Huber in the passage last cited—in disciplinam juris gentium abiit, ut civitas alterius civitatis leges apud se valere patiatur. It is, however, evident, from the remarks in the *Prælectiones* following the three maxims, that he there conceived that the tribunals were to base their recognition and allowance of the effects of foreign laws upon considerations of comity, reciprocal utility, &c. And in saying in that place that the three maxims, or this topic of jurisprudence, belongs to the *jus gentium*, and not the *jus civile*, he apparently intends, by the former, that international law of which nations, in their political personality, are the subjects.[2]

---

[1] So in 1 Voet, de Statutis, § 1; 12, 17. "Dein quid ex comitate gens genti ... liberaliter et officiose indulgeat, permittat, patiatur, ultro citroque."

[2] It will be necessary, hereinafter, to show that the term *jus gentium*, in the writings of the civilians, has been used in two significations, the one being the original meaning which it has in the Corpus Juris Civilis, equivalent to *universal jurisprudence* the other, a modern meaning equivalent to *public international law*, according to the definitions given in the first chapter. This double meaning has occasioned much misconception and misquotation. See Reddie's Inq. Elem. &c., ch. iv.

§ 81. The later writers following Huber have constantly cited the axiom as implying that judicial tribunals are to regard the comity of nations and considerations of reciprocal advantage as a criterion by which they are to allow or disallow the operation of foreign laws upon persons and things within the jurisdiction of their states; or—to vary the form of statement—that the tribunals are to take into consideration whether out of comity, or by, or for, or under comity, the nation or state is bound to admit the operation of the foreign laws, and then determine the rights and obligations of private persons accordingly.

This idea of a *judicial* recognition of comity of nations, reciprocal advantage, &c.,—the motives which are supposed to act on the supreme authority—the rector imperii, seems to have been seized upon from an inability to discover what authority a judicial tribunal could have in making that practical recognition of the effects of foreign laws which it was plainly seen was nevertheless constantly taking place. In order to justify the courts in thus giving effect, as it seemed, to a foreign law, the courts were made to assume the powers of the state or of the sovereign. They were supposed to have abandoned their judicial function of applying the national law (positive law) to private persons, and to have assumed to act for the state in its political legislative capacity, and to decide what were the dictates and requirements of a rule which, in operating on the state as its subject, is a public law, and a law in the imperfect sense only: while, in fact, neither comity nor any other motive or rule acting on states or nations had anything to do with the *judicial* recognition or non-recognition of the foreign law. The state, in vesting the tribunal with juridical power, and having recognized all other states as expository of that rule of right which was to be enforced in its own jurisdiction as positive law, had already recognized the validity of the effects of foreign laws within its own jurisdiction, if not contrary to the rule of right contained in its own local municipal (internal) law, and this question of contrariety was the only one for the consideration of the tribunal.

The whole of this doctrine of the comity of the nation applied by the court,[1] involves the fallacy that the tribunal is to determine the rule of right for the action of the state, when the whole of jurisprudence is founded on the principle that the state determines the rule of right for the action of the tribunal.

§ 82. Judge Story, in his Conflict of Laws, § 31, accepts Huber's three maxims for the basis of private international law, but it will be seen that in translating the third maxim he introduces the word *ought* in a manner not strictly justified by the terms of the original; though, by so wording it, the real basis of the action of judicial tribunals is indicated. The maxim as given by Story, Confl. of L., § 29, is: "The rulers of every empire, from comity, admit that the laws of every people in force within its own limits, ought to have the same force every where, so far as they do not prejudice the powers or rights of other governments, or of their citizens." In Huber's statement, it is not said that the *rectores imperii* admit that foreign laws *ought* to have effect, or that it is *right* that they should have effect, &c. It is merely said that, in point of fact, they have allowed them to take effect. But the *practice* thus stated by Huber is, to the tribunal of the forum of jurisdiction, the indication that the national law—or the author of the national law, does consider that foreign laws ought to have that effect; and

---

[1] 13 Peters R., 589, by Taney, C. J., citing Story's Confl. of L., § 38. "It is not the comity of the court, but the comity of the nation, which is administered and ascertained in the same way, and guided by the same reasoning by which all other principles of municipal law are ascertained and guided." 1 Greenleaf Evid., § 43.

Therefore, the idea of "comity of nations," "international comity," operating as a judicial rule, has been denominated by some authors a fiction of romance. Schæffner, §§ 29, 30, says: "From being jurists they became poets; inventing the fiction, that the comity of the nation was making place for the foreign law: or else—in instances of direct juridical contradiction between the two laws—they played the part of the statesman instead of that of the jurist; pointing out the commercial or other disadvantages which might accrue to the subjects of their own state if the foreign law should be disallowed.

"This romantic idea of the *comitas gentium*, originating in a misconception of the nature of law, and bearing a great resemblance to a *blocus hermétique*, lurks in many of the older treatises, and reappears even at the present day, as, for example, in Story's work. Now, if we observe closely how the principle of the *comitas gentium* has been carried out, we become aware, to our surprise, that it has never, in fact, been actually applied, or at least that in most of the supposed cases, some principle entirely distinct from the *comitas* has been appealed to. How could any consistent result be attained by following a conception so utterly vague and unjuristical. It is not possible, in fact, even approximately, to decide correctly the simplest question of international private law by this principle. Where is the beginning of the end of comity? How can questions of law be answered according to political considerations which are of all others the most fluctuating?" (Transl.)

therefore, it is also to that tribunal its authorization in realizing or maintaining the rights and obligations belonging to the relation created by the foreign law. If the state to which the tribunal belongs had not indicated its approval of this customary action of states or nations, the court or tribunal would have no power, from the practice here stated, to maintain the effects of foreign laws: whatever view it might take of the demands of international comity, and the prospect of reciprocal advantage. This indication is found in the customary law of such state; which, as has been shown in the first chapter, § 36, recognizes other civilized states or nations as the legitimate expositors of natural reason, and requires its tribunals to recognize a universal jurisprudence, a historical *law of nations*, ascertained from the practice of all civilized nations. The motives for that practice are immaterial. It is the customary law of the land, derived from the legislative and juridical practice of nations, having an international effect, which the tribunal applies under this rule; not the considerations of duty or of advantage which may be supposed to operate on states and nations in regulating their conduct by any code of law, so called.

§ 83. M. Fœlix, in his Droit International Privé, ch. iii., Principes Fondamentaux, note, professes entire concurrence with Judge Story's view of the principle of comity. " Le doctrine que nous exposons dans ce chapitre est celle de M. Story; nous l'adoptons complétement." And he expressly vindicates, the doctrine of a comity of nations—international comity applicable by the tribunals; that is, makes the question—what does comity require? a question for courts of law to decide. In §11, his language is—" Les legislateurs, les authorités publiques, les tribunaux et les auteurs, en admettant l'application des lois étrangères, se dirigent non pas d'après un devoir de nécessité, d'après une obligation dont l'execution peut être exigée, mais uniquement d'après des considerations de utilité et de convenance réciproque entre les nations (ex comitate gentium, ob reciprocam utilitatem,") &c.—going on to describe the motives which may and do operate on sovereign states, in allowing a foreign law to operate: but making no distinction between the functions of the judge and the legislator, and as appears in the citation here given, even putting administrative officers—*les autorités publiques*, and the publicists—*les auteurs*, all in the same juridical position.

In another part of the same section, M. Fœlix speaks of the force of the practice of nations in this respect as a juridical authority; meaning, apparently, that this practice is the warrant for the admission or application of foreign laws by judicial tribunals.—" Mais ce qu'il y a de certain c'est qu'aujourd'hui toutes les nations ont adopté *en principe*, l'application dans leurs territoires des lois étrangères, sauf toutefois les restrictions exigées par le droit de souveraineté et de l'intérêt de leur propres sujets." And near the end of the chapter—" L'usage des nations a établi, *pour leur avantage réciproque*, et dans certains cas, l'effet des lois étrangères;" without, however, stating explicitly whether the tribunal is bound to regulate its decisions by this "usage des nations," or is to consider comity and "avantage réciproque," before making the allowance.

§ 84. If it were simply stated that the custom of nations having been *comiter*—that is, either in a way which shows comity and good will, or prompted by comity and the hope of reciprocal advantage, to require their judicial tribunals to maintain the relations created by foreign laws when not contrary to the rule of right established by the local law, or, in the language of Huber—" quatenus nihil potestati et juri alterius imperantis aut ejusdem civium præjudicetur;" or, in the language of M. Fœlix—"sauf toutefois les restrictions exigées par le droit de souveraineté et de l'intérêt de leur propres sujets,"— therefore the tribunals of any one nation are bound to carry out or maintain the relations created by foreign laws, there would be no practical objection to the allegation that the political cause of that admission is the good will of the nation and the prospect of reciprocal benefit; and there would be very little practical utility in the attempt which has here been made to discriminate the true theory of the *judicial* recognition of foreign laws. The question before the tribunal would, under either view, practically be decided by the same inquiry—that is, whether the relation created by the foreign law is contrary to the rule of right—*potestati et juri* contained in the local law, as before explained. But it is evident that the effect of basing the historical fact of this customary *judicial* recognition upon comity has been to induce judges to assume the part of diplomatists, acting for the state or nation in its integral political personality, and to decide matters of private right (the rights and obligations of private persons) by political considerations. And there is much in the writings of Story, Fœlix, and others, to sanction this practice.

This tendency, which is no where more apparent than in the juridical literature of the United States, has in a great degree been caused by the supposed necessity of a judicial protest against another misconception, entertained by some few writers on these questions, who hold that a state may be *bound* (as if by positive law) to admit foreign laws to operate within its territory, if not actually injurious to its political sovereignty. Story, Conf. of L. § 33, observes, " It has been thought by some jurists that the term 'comity' is not sufficiently expressive of the obligation of nations to give effect to foreign laws when they are not prejudicial to their own rights and interests. And it has been suggested that the doctrine rests on a deeper foundation; that it is not so much a matter of comity, or courtesy, as a matter of paramount moral duty," (citing Livermore: Dissertation on the contrariety of laws, p. 26 to p. 30.) But these jurists also make this supposed duty of the state the basis of the action of the tribunal. Now, the duty of the state is evidently beyond the action of its own judicial officers. The admission, to whatever degree it may be sanctioned by the state, may have resulted from motives of comity, or from a sense of duty. But if comity, or any thing else, is conceived of as a necessarily binding measure of the degree in which this *judicial admission* shall take place, then a rule, operating as positive law, is assumed to have determined the juridical action of the state, when, in jurisprudence—the science of what law *is,* the action of the state is the only possible criterion of the rule. The comity of nations, operating as *law* within any one national jurisdiction, will be only whatever the possessor of supreme legislative power therein allows for comity, or by comity.

Jurists, who, on the other hand, have asserted that absolute independence of the state in this matter which is a necessary consequence of fundamental principles, have apparently been unable to distinguish between the different positions of *the state* (acting under a law of the imperfect kind) and *the tribunal* (authorized only to apply positive law): not remembering that though the state is not bound to admit the foreign law, yet its tribunals may be bound to admit it or recognize its effects; though they are bound to do so, and can do so, only so far as the state may have indicated its will on the point. Therefore, in proposing to enforce that rule which the state *has sanctioned* as right, the tribunals have conceived themselves as determining also what the state *ought to sanction* as right. Or, to resort to the language of German (Kantian) metaphysics, the law they have applied in these cases has been a *subjective* and not an *objective* conception of the rule of action.[1]

[1] Waechter, on the Collision of the private laws of different States, (Archiv. f. d. Civil. Pr. B. 24, p. 238.) Transl.

"It is agreed on all hands, and our laws unmistakeably declare, that the law derives its validity from itself, from the moment of its being formally promulgated, unconditionally, and without reference to the *subjective* opinion of individual members of the state in respect to its intrinsic merit and accordance with justice; that the requisition of a constitutional form and the limits of a constitutional power alone determine its validity, and not the nature of a law according to *subjective* theories. The judge is simply the instrument of legislative will, declared in a certain formally legal manner, (the common will, to which each individual will in the state must be unconditionally subject) and this law it is the province of the judge to apply, without considering whether it is just or unjust, suitable or unsuitable, conformable or not conformable, in his *subjective* conception, to the nature of a law; and the citizen is equally bound to submit himself to this general will. If, for example, the law of a state expressly determines according to which rule a relation created in a foreign country is to be adjudicated—whether by the local law of the *forum*, or by that of the foreign country, the judge in that state is bound to decide accordingly; even if such adjudication may in itself be called inconvenient, unjust, or contrary to the natural requisitions of a law. * * * * The possessor of legislative power, in making a statutory determination of the question, will regard it from two several points of view; considering on the one side—the interests of the local juridical system, the exclusion therefrom of discordant elements and the maintenance of injunctions based on high purposes and the requisites of a jural society, and of the dignity and independence of its juridical power;—on the other side—the considerations of international justice which here become operative, and which demand the recognition of the legal capacity of the foreigner as well as that of the citizen, and also, in many instances, make the allowance of foreign laws advisable.— But though these considerations of utility, reasonableness, friendly understanding, natural law and the like may, and in a certain degree ought to influence the legislator, especially in forming international compacts respecting these questions, these are not matters for a judicial officer to take into consideration. He has only to inquire what the juridical will of his sovereign or the positive law of his own state may have determined on these points." And, in a note, "The different positions of the judicial officer and of the legislator are too often confounded, in treating of this topic of jurisprudence."

Savigny, Heut. R. R., B. 3, c. 1, § 348, citing this passage from Waechter, thinks

§ 85. But, irrespectively of the method or principle by which the judicial tribunal will have authority, in any case, to recognize and maintain relations created by foreign laws,—before the maxim as herein before stated, (§ 77,) or as stated by Huber and Story, can be practically applied by a tribunal supposed to have jurisdiction of an alien, that tribunal must be furnished with a test by which to know in what cases the foreign law, if allowed to take effect, would conflict with the *potestas* and *jus*—" the *power* or *rights* of its own government and its citizens." Or, according to the translation herein before given, (§ 80) of the word *jus* and the *a priori* view taken of the foundation for the international admission of foreign laws, (§ 77,) that tribunal, —admitting the presumption to be in favor of their admission— must still compare the foreign law with the *measure of right* contained in the local law,—its own municipal or internal law. In this connexion the *potestas* and *jus* of a state may be taken to be equivalent to its public and private municipal law, which are necessarily taken in its own courts to be *jural* rules,—rules accordant with natural right or natural reason.

§ 86. Laws which differ in their national source and character, may be called the same or similar laws, when each, within its own jurisdiction, produces similar correlative rights and obligations between persons in similar circumstances of natural condition. Any two such laws, must, in that case, be taken by the tribunals of the respective authors of each to be equally correspondent with natural reason; or, to change the form of expression, rights and obligations so produced by one national law, must be taken, in the jurisdiction of the other national law, to be correspondent with natural reason. And if the persons and things who are the subjects and objects of these rights and obligations pass from the jurisdiction of one law to that of another, the foreign law may be taken, by the tribunals of the latter, to be consistent with the *potestas* and *jus* of the latter—following the terms of Huber's maxim: and the

it too restrictive of the judicial function: Savigny attributing a greater relative importance to judicial tribunals as a source of law. But compare Fœlix: Dr. Internat. Pr., Pref. v. vi. n, on the importance in juristical literature of distinguishing between *a priori* and *a posteriori* doctrines.

foreign law be allowed international recognition and support; having then, in fact, a personal extent in a new forum.[1]

§ 87. Every national law is necessarily taken, by its own author and tribunals, to be rightful in the circumstances and for the persons to whom it is applied. But even if laws of different national origin should, each in its own jurisdiction, create different relations from those which would be created by the other, in the jurisdiction of that other, in reference to similar persons and things, (in which case the two laws could not be said to agree in a judgment of the dictates of natural reason), yet it does not follow of necessity that they are *opposed* in such judgment, or that the tribunals of either jurisdiction should deny a jural character to the laws of the other, operating in the jurisdiction of that other, or that either should refuse to acknowledge any of the effects and consequences of the law of that other, in the relations of persons formerly subject thereto, who might afterwards pass under or be found within its own jurisdiction. For though every principle entering into the municipal (internal) law of a state must be taken by its tribunals to be a jural law, and accordant with natural reason, it is, in the nature of the case, first promulgated as a law for persons and things within its several territorial jurisdiction.[2] But when any distinction of persons as alien or domiciled is made then the question of *the extent* of the principles of the local (internal) law, is to be determined judicially; looking to the intention of the supreme power. For a principle of the local law may be intended to apply to one or more specified persons, or to a class of persons, or to all persons indifferently, within the jurisdiction. It may be intended to affect the relations of those persons only who are domiciled or native subjects, or of those only who are aliens to the jurisdiction, or it may apply to all human beings generally, as the objects and agents of that action in a civil state which the law

---

[1] See *ante*, §§ 53–56.

[2] "For there are in nature certain fountains of justice whence all civil laws are derived, but as streams; and like as waters do take tinctures and tastes from the soil through which they run, so do civil laws vary according to the regions and governments where they are planted, though they proceed from the same fountain." Bacon Adv. Learn. B. II. c 8. Works, vol. I. 238. Am. Ed.

Montesquieu: Spirit of Laws, Book I, c. 3.

Scaccia: Tractatus de Commer., Quæst. VII. par. II. ampl. 19, § 19.

contemplates. The judicial officer, while enforcing the local law as the rule of right, must apply it according to the limitations and with the extent intended by the supreme sovereign will. And in the jurisprudence of every state its own laws may be distinguished as being jural, either by being merely expedient and suitable to circumstances of position and character peculiar to itself, or jural by enforcing obligations founded on the nature of man and co-extensive with human existence; (though this distinction is the growth of an advanced stage of jurisprudence, as will be shown.) In other words, although the municipal (internal) law of any nation is always to be taken as a rule of right for its own national domain, it does not follow that it has been asserted by its author for a rule of universal obligation, or as the rule which ought to be everywhere applied to persons and things in like circumstances; in such a sense that the tribunals of that nation are bound to consider every rule contrary to natural reason which should produce effects unknown to the local law.

§ 88. When, therefore, we pass beyond that portion of international law which consists in necessary axiomatic principles, recognized in the very existence of states or nations (and which includes the three axiomatic maxims herein before given, § 63, 67,) to that portion which becomes a rule of action and a law in the primary sense for judicial tribunals, in making that international recognition and allowance of foreign laws which is only *supposed* in the third of those maxims, that part which, though dependent for its force as law upon the autonomous and uncontrolled action of single states, and therefore, not a law in the strict sense for the state, is yet a law in the strict sense for the judicial tribunal and for private persons—private international law, included in the *national* law of the forum—the first, or simplest general principle which may be stated for such law, seems to be this:—*That relations of persons and their constituent rights and obligations, existing under the law and jurisdiction of one state are to be judicially admitted to international recognition (that is, be allowed to have legal effect) within the jurisdiction of other states, when they are not inconsistent with those principles which in the jurisdiction of the latter are juridically known as* *principles of universal personal application and extent, or which the local law applies to all natural persons within its power and territorial jurisdiction.*¹ And this will include the test for the admission of foreign laws, which is implied in Huber's third maxim—the *power* and *law of right,—potestas* and *jus,* of the nation; or that given by Story's version of the same as the limits of comity,—"the known policy and interest" of the state in which is supposed to be the forum of jurisdiction. For the power (sovereignty) and jural character of a state lie at the foundation of its whole law, public or private, constituting the objects of its existence as a part of political society, which are considered by it in the minutest application of law, and must be judicially regarded as the policy and interest of every state, which it maintains wherever it acts as a source of law, or which it applies to all persons within its jurisdiction.

This principle so stated may be regarded as law,—in the sense of a rule of action which is applicable by judicial tribunals; though, in the nature of the case, it cannot acquire the force of a rule to which the state is subject, as under a law in the strict and proper sense of the word. And though, under this rule, the foreign law may be said to produce legal effects, the authority which gives it its coercive force over private persons and the legislative will which directs the tribunal to apply it is always that of the nation having supreme power in the forum. Therefore, the law which causes the legal effect to be realized or actualized is not the law of the foreign country, but that of the forum.² The law of the foreign country does not operate in the forum, but it is only a fact or circumstance upon which the local juridical power operates; and therefore the foreign law is always to be proved like any other fact.³

§ 89. But since there may be recognized exceptions to the extent of every general rule, there may, in any one jurisdiction, be a person or persons whose relations to other persons and to

---

¹ The rule given by Schæffner, § 22, for the most general one, may be translated, "Each legal relation is to be adjudicated according to the law of the state wherein it has become existent. (wo es existent geworden ist.) And with this, regard must be paid to those laws whose whole design is to cause a legal relation to be recognized as such only when it accords with those laws."
² See *ante,* § 67, and note.   ³ See *ante,* § 74.

things are, by force of certain local circumstances, regarded by the supreme power as being specially exempt from the operation of rules or principles to which, irrespectively of those local circumstances, a universal personal extent is attributed ; and in this case, notwithstanding the actual exception, under the law of the *forum*, (the internal law,) to the universal extent of these rules or principles, they must still, in their otherwise universal extent, be judicially applied to limit the effects of foreign laws in the manner above indicated.

§ 90. But if a relation may thus have a jural existence in a certain national jurisdiction, though contrary to principles having an otherwise universal personal extent, there might, in other countries, be legal relations which, though contrary to the same principles, should be equally accordant with natural reason in and for the local circumstances of such other countries. And when the persons who sustained rights and obligations in those relations have passed into other dominions, in which the universal personal extent of a principle having a contrary effect will prevent their continuance, still the action arising out of those relations may be regarded as having been lawful in their original *forum*—the *forum domicilii*—though in the new *forum*—the *forum of jurisdiction*, they can no longer continue.

§ 91. The effect of laws having this universal extent must be, like that of every other, to create relations and to attribute rights and their correlative duties, (§ 22.) The rights so attributed by these laws must be in either individual (absolute) or relative. But rights ordinarily known as relative are the attributes of particular persons, in specific relations to other particular persons, (§ 40.) A legal capacity for those rights, which is in itself, in some sense, an individual right, may be universally attributed ; though, in the nature of the case, the same relative rights cannot be attributed to all. Individual or absolute rights, however, which exist in relations of one individual to all persons in the community in which such individual may be found, may be attributed to all persons constituting that community. The laws, therefore, which, in having universal personal extent, control the international admission of the effects of foreign laws in reference to the *status* of private persons, will principally be such as attribute some individual right with its correspondent obligations.

§ 92. This international comparison of foreign laws with the local or municipal law and a universally applicable rule of right contained therein, must always be, in its earliest occurrence, an autonomic discrimination on the part of the tribunal. That is, supposing such international question to have arisen for the first time, it would depend upon the unsupported moral sense—the conscientious judgment of the tribunal, (*arbitrium boni viri*,) in the absence of any positive legislation: every such judgment becoming, of course, a precedent and a law for succeeding tribunals, acting under the same national authority; by which, in course of time, an ascertained customary private international law arises, in and for that jurisdiction.

This juridical act of admitting or rejecting the effects of foreign laws, on the ground of their being repugnant or otherwise to principles of the local law, which are applicable to *all* persons in certain circumstances of natural condition, is, strictly speaking, the act of judicial tribunals only. It is, however, in a certain degree, conceivable as being the act of a legislator also. (See *post*, § 102.)

§ 93. But, in whatever way manifested, this juridical action, when it has taken place on the part of various nations, forms one of those criteria by which the tribunals of any one state may determine what principles, or rules, shall be taken to be rightful, or rules accordant with natural reason, and applicable as the presumptive will of the state under whose authority they act; and also to determine the personal extent of those rules: that is, in the absence of positive legislation, or of precedents of local origin, (*ante*, § 33.) And it is to be observed that, in making this discrimination of laws which shall have a personal extent and international recognition in some other jurisdiction than that in which they were first enforced, the practice of other nations in similar cases has a more original and intrinsic force, as an *international* precedent, (or a precedent of private *international* law,) for the tribunals of any one state, than foreign law and jurisprudence has, as an exposition of right in cases falling under the department of *municipal* (internal) law. Because it is only by supposing the existence of independent jurisdictions, and a judgment of the tribunals of one, in allowing or disallowing the effects of another's laws, that there can be any exemplification of a judgment, by the recognized interpreters of the will of states, deciding what effects produced by the laws of one state are incompatible with the power and law of right—*potestas et jus*—of another, and what principles of the law of particular states are to be taken to have universal personal extent under the jurisdiction of those states, or constant application to all persons in certain circumstances of natural condition.

§ 94. But in the continuous repetition of similar judgments by the tribunals and legislators of different nations through a long period of time, and the mutual reference made by them to such judgments; together with the customarily received comments of private writers of various nations upon the same, based upon the idea that such judgments contain an exposition of natural reason, some principles, from being constantly recognized by many different nations, will acquire, in the jurisprudence of any one nation, the known character of *universal principles*, or principles of *a universal jurisprudence*. For though, taking law in the strict sense of the word, jurisprudence is the science of the law of some one country or nation, (§ 18,) yet, by distinguishing (national) law into municipal (internal) and international, and by the application of the latter to the relations of persons formerly subject to foreign jurisdictions, a portion of the jurisprudence of each country will be identified with the science of a *universal law*, or *law of nations*. This, though dependent on the supreme national power for its continuance, or coercive effect within the jurisdiction of that nation, may yet, by its tribunals, be considered principles presumed to have universal territorial extent and obligation, and to have legal force distinct from those rules or laws which the state may promulgate as originating in its own separate juridical or legislative power: which last, though equally jural,—or equally intended to conform to natural reason,—are promulgated as law for one dominion only, or, rather, for persons as being simply the inhabitants of its own jurisdiction, without reference to the existence of other similar jurisdictions; and they have, consequently, a peculiar local or territorial character; as have also the relations created by those laws.

The legislative (juridical) authority by which any principles, having this universal character in the history of jurisprudence, are recognized by the tribunal as being accordant with natural reason, and allowed to determine the relations of alien persons, is, indeed, that of the state within whose limits such aliens may be found, and that recognition is ultimately dependent on the political possessor of the supreme civil power. But this is not inconsistent with the assertion, that in the progress of jurisprudence among different nations, a portion of the law of each may be said to result from the general promulgation of all nations, the effects of which its judicial tribunals will recognize without reference to their own national sovereign as the source or origin of law, though such effects are still known to depend in each jurisdiction upon the will of the supreme power, and are recognized and accepted with the intention of carrying out that will.[1] Or, making use of the language of the Institutes, it may be said, that the interpretation of law as a rule of right, and one founded in natural reason,—quod naturalis ratio inter omnes homines constituit—has been, as matter of history, so uniform in respect to some relations of persons, and has been so frequently and so harmoniously applied as private international law, that it may be known as that law which inter omnes populos peræque custoditur:—a *jus gentium*,—a law among nations, or universal law; the effects of which may be

---

[1] Savigny: Heut. Rom. R., B. i., c. 3, § 22. Tr.: "In the commencement of their intercourse with the neighboring foreign states it became necessary for the Roman tribunals to recognize, together with their own national law, a law applicable to foreigners; and not merely the law of some one foreign state, but that which was common to a number of such states. By the extension of the Roman dominion, and the greater diversity of their intercourse with foreigners, their field of view in this respect became proportionately enlarged, and in this manner they gradually conceived the more abstract idea of a law common to the Romans together with all nations, or all mankind. It is evident that the Romans, in founding this conception on observation, could not but have seen that their induction was imperfect, because they did not know every nation, and it is certain that they never were careful to ascertain whether their *jus gentium* actually obtained in the laws of all those that they did know. Still it was natural, after recognizing this comparative universality, to go back to its source, and this they found to be, universally, in naturalis ratio; i. e., the consciousness, implanted in the common nature of man, of a moral rule."

See also, Hist. of Rom. L. in the Middle Age, by the same author; Cathcart's Tr.,

particularly enumerated, as is done in the Institutes, Lib. I., tit. ii., § 2. Ex hoc jure gentium omnes pæne contractus introducti sunt, ut emtio, venditio, locatio, conductio, societas, depositum, mutuum et alii innumerabiles. And in the jurisprudence of every nation the law may be distinguished as being either rules peculiar to itself, jus civile or *proprium*, or else rules common to it with the rest of mankind, jus *gentium;* each of which divisions of the law (national law,—jus civile in that sense) may be applied as international or as municipal (internal) law: that is, may be applied either to alien or to domiciled subjects. The term "law of nations" has, in modern jurisprudence, been generally taken to mean public international law only: but the original use of the term, in Roman jurisprudence, as will be hereinafter more fully shown, (ch. iv.,) was that of a private law universally recognized.[1]

§ 95. And though these principles of a so called universal jurisprudence have that character from the historical fact that the relations created by them have been found in force among all nations, and therefore must be supposed to be already known effects of the local (internal) law of each single nation,[2] yet they may retain their jural character and be judicially recognized and applied, on the ground of their historical universality, even when none of the domiciled inhabitants of the forum sustain such relations under the municipal (internal) law.

Having once acquired the character of jural rules, in the jurisprudence of each state, by an *a posteriori* or *inductive* method, —i. e. from the fact of their general recognition,—they will thereafter obtain and operate as *a priori* principles,—or principles from which consequences are to be drawn *deductively*, and will be judicially recognized, by the tribunals of any one nation, because having this character.[3]

§ 96. Therefore when persons who sustain legal relations under the legislative or juridical authority of some state of dom-

---

ch. i., § 1; and in Fœlix: Dr. Int. Pr., § 122, a recognition of this feature of the Roman law; contrasting it with a remarkable difference in this respect, in the modern French international jurisprudence.

[1] Compare *ante*, § 34, and notes.

[2] Quod civile non idem continuo gentium; quod autem gentium idem civile esse debet. Cicero de Off. III. 17. Gaius, ap. Dig. Lib. I. Tit. i. § 9.

[3] Peckius, de Regulis Juris, 1.

icil, appear as aliens within any other national jurisdiction, those relations, and the rights and obligations in which they consist, will be recognized, allowed, sustained or maintained, by the judicial tribunals within that jurisdiction, when such anterior relations were founded on principles which have this universal character in the history of jurisprudence; without instituting *de novo* a comparison of those relations with the effects of the local (internal) law: and they will be internationally supported as consistent with the *power, law and right*—potestate et jure—of the state having jurisdiction; until positively disallowed by the will of the supreme national power, to be ascertained by some known judicial method.[1] In fact when the anterior relations of aliens are thus continued by the recognition of the historical universality of the legal rule from which they arise, that recognition is an application of *international* private law only from the character or position of the persons to whom those relations are ascribed. But there is in this case no *conflict* between the laws of the two *forums* or jurisdictions, nor any occasion to suppose the operation of international comity,—the comity of the nation. For in this case, by the recognition of the universal prevalence of these principles, the relations so sustained may be said to derive their support directly from the municipal (national) law of the *forum*—the same law, in its legislative source and authority, as that which determines the relations of domiciled inhabitants; for being principles of a *universal* jurisprudence they must be supposed to form a part of that law.[2] But

---

[1] Thus in Scrimshire *vs.* Scrimshire, 2 Hagg. Cons. Rep. p. 421, it is said, "As there is no positive law of this country which prohibits the court from taking notice of the *jus gentium.*"

Greenl. Evid. I. § 5. "In like manner the law of nations and the general customs and usages of merchants, as well as the general law and customs of our own country, are recognized without proof by the courts of all civilized nations." (Citing 2 Ld. Raymond, 1542, Heineccius ad Pand. 1. 22, tit. 3, sec. 119. 1 Bl. Comm. 75, 76, 85.) —Here the same universal jurisprudence seems intended, though the term "law of nations" is probably conceived of as being public rather than private law.

[2] Scrimshire *vs.* Scrimshire, 2 Hagg. Consistory R. p. 417. "The *jus gentium* is the law of every country; every country takes notice of it, and this court, observing that law in determining upon this case, cannot be said to determine English rights by the law of France, but by the law of England, of which the *jus gentium* is a part."— Here the term *jus gentium*—law of *nations*, is used in its original signification—that of private law,—a law determining the relations of private persons, which is known by its universal reception. There are many other cases in which the law of nations is said to be part of the law of England, when, by that term, public international law—the rule acting on nations as political persons is intended: Bl. Comm. I. p. 273,

since it is only by the recognition of some persons as aliens, or as having before sustained relations which did not, in the first instance, *exist* under the legislative authority of the country to which they are alien, that such discrimination can be made, it is only, or primarily at least only, in international law that this universal law or jurisprudence can be recognized.[1]

When any principles of universal jurisprudence have been thus recognized and applied, in the international law of any particular jurisdiction, to determine the condition of alien persons, they will also form a part of the municipal (internal) law of the same jurisdiction, if the alien persons, or those formerly subject to the national law of another domicil, acquire a new domicil in that jurisdiction. Being received as an authoritative exposition of natural reason, with the extent of a personal law, (§ 27,) they must be held to be equally authoritative to determine the condition of the same persons in the *forum* to which they are transferred whether they retain or lose their former domicil.

§ 97. But however general that recognition of any rule of action may have been among the various states or nations of the world, it is not a universal law in the sense of being a judicial rule within the jurisdiction of every state independently of its own will or consent. The word *universal* is a term here applied to a rule or principle in respect of its historical prevalence, and not in respect to an intrinsic universal authority; its actual force, before the tribunals of any state, lying only in the judi-

---

IV. p. 67. Triquet *v.* Bath, 3, Burr. 1480. Respub. *v.* Longchamps, 1, Dall. 111. The admiralty Reports, *passim ;* but this latter use is not proper; except in the consideration that public international law always involves, to a certain extent, the relations of private persons.

[1] Thus the law of maritime commerce prevailing in some one country consists in a great degree in the *law of nations*, or universal jurisprudence ; because it must, in a great measure, be formed by the judicial application of private international law; or, in other words, because in point of fact, those relations of private persons which are known in maritime commerce, generally involve actions which must take place in some other jurisdiction than that in which the correlative rights and obligations arising out of those relations have been enforced or are to be enforced.

Kaimes, Princip. of Eq. B. III. c. 8. "Thus in the Kingdom of Scotland, all foreign matters were formerly heard and decided on by the King in council; in later times a special jurisdiction has been vested for that purpose in the court of Sessions, which decides all such causes on general principles of Equity."

Gaius : Com. I. § 92, calls the jus gentium :—" Leges moresque peregrinorum ; " see also Reddie : Hist. View of the Law of marit. Com. p. 82, 118. Waechter, Arch. f. d. Civil. Prax. Bd. 24, p. 245–6. Smith's Dict. Antiq. *voc.*—Prætor.

cial presumption that such principle is accordant with natural reason, and that the state, therefore, intends to enforce it as law.[1]

If the state, or those who hold the supreme power thereof, have promulgated any principles with a universal personal extent, i. e. an application to all natural persons within its jurisdiction, which are contrary to the principles of the law historically known as universal, or which produce opposite effects, the tribunal is bound to apply those principles of its own local law, as a test of the accordance of foreign laws with natural reason, without regard to the principles of universal jurisprudence—the *law of nations*—thus historically known.[2]

§ 98. It must be carefully noted that, in this inquiry into the principles regulating the admission or the exclusion of the effect of foreign laws, the term *universal* is applied to legal principles in reference to two entirely distinct incidents of their existence. In the one case the qualitative term *universal* is used with reference to the anterior reception of a legal principle among *all nations*, or at least all nations that are considered, by the state under which the tribunal acts, as sufficiently enlightened to be authoritative exponents of natural reason (§ 36). In the other case the same term is employed with reference to the application of a legal principle to *all individuals* within the power or jurisdiction of some one state, nation, or possessor of

---

[1] The historical *law of nations*, the universal jurisprudence thus manifested in international law, is therefore the natural law, so far as it can be recognized in jurisprudence, (ante § 34–36). The following passage from Long's Discourses, p. 62, is a modification from that before given from Savigny; but it is here inserted as showing the modern apprehension of the jus gentium:

"The observation of those rules of law in their own system which were of a general character and not peculiarly Roman, and the comparison of them with like rules of law which obtained in other states, may have led the Romans to a consideration of those universal principles which prevail in the laws of all nations. In matters in dispute between aliens and Romans, they must also have been led to a practical acquaintance with the law of foreign states, and to the reception of such law, when it was recommended by reasons of utility, and when it was not opposed to the positive rules of their own Jus Civile. As the Romans were a practical, and not a theoretical, people, it seems that it was in this way, by their intercourse with other people, that they were led to the assumption or the acceptance of the notion of rules of law more general than the strict Roman rules. This was the probable origin of the notion of a Jus Gentium, or Jus Naturale or natural law, which two terms are perfectly equivalent in the Roman writers. The term Jus Gentium has a reference to the mode in which the notion originated, that is, from the intercourse with other states; the Jus Naturale is the term more applicable to the induction, when made more complete by further acquaintance with the institutions of other people, and by the development of more universal notions."

[2] See *ante*, § 77, and § 88.

sovereign national power, from whom the principle derives its coercive force. For while it is evident that no state has of itself any power to establish a new principle in universal jurisprudence—the historical *law of nations*, (i. e., the law whose universality is a historical fact,) which, from having that character, is receivable by the tribunals of any one country as being presumptively accordant with natural reason every where, yet, within its own territory and jurisdiction, it may attribute to any principle the character of a law which is to be applied *universally*,—that is, applied by its own judicial tribunals to *all persons*, within its own jurisdiction, in certain circumstances of natural condition, or as one founded on the nature of individual men forming the constituents of society; whether it be consonant or not with the code of universal law, or *the law of nations*, historically known.

§ 99. Although, therefore, in the course of the international recognition of the effects of foreign laws, and of the general progress of jurisprudence among civilized nations, some relations, rights and obligations of alien persons, or more generally,—of persons before subject to other jurisdictions,—are, from their general prevalence among nations, as proved by history, to be judicially allowed therein, as accordant with natural reason, or as jural relations,—yet that recognition will always be limited by whatever principles in the municipal (internal) law of the forum of jurisdiction, may have a *universal personal* extent, or apply to all persons under that jurisdiction in certain circumstances of natural condition; being promulgated by the supreme source of the local law as principles which ought to apply to all natural persons in such circumstances.

It being here asserted that the judicial recognition and admission of the effects of foreign laws on a presumptive accordance with natural reason, (*ante* § 77,) is always limited by the operation of local laws having universal personal extent, it may be objected, that this reference to a universal jurisprudence—the historical *law of nations*, in the application of private international law, is of no actual force; and that is sufficient to say, that relations existent under foreign laws are always to be judicially maintained, on the principle of comity, (so called,) unless the local law having universal personal extent produces rights and obligations inconsistent with those relations. But the validity of this reference is found in the fact that the personal extent of laws,—the question whether they are universal or limited, is ordinarily determined, (as is the far greater part of all positive law,) by judicial action; and that this is to be in the mode in which any rule of law is judicially determined: that is, from external indices of natural reason already accepted by the state; of which universal jurisprudence—the *law of nations*, must always be one. And here is shown the genital connection of universal jurisprudence, or the *law of nations*, with that part of the laws of each country which is universally applied,— has universal personal extent, so far as the legislative or juridical power of that country extends. For the actual universal jurisprudence—the historical *law of nations*—grows out of, or is discernible by the discrimination, (under private international law,) of a part of the law of each nation having universal personal extent, and constituting a standard, in its own courts of law, of the accordance of foreign laws with natural reason.[1]

§ 100. It may also be objected that it is a contradiction in terms to recognize a principle as forming part of the *law of nations*, or as being a principle of *universal* jurisprudence, and at the same time to intimate a possibility of its being contravened by the local law; for if it is not recognized in the local law it is not *universally* received; or is not part of the laws of *all* nations. Strictly speaking, this is true. Yet it is evident that the sovereign legislative power may contravene principles which before were universally received, or which in the history of jurisprudence have before had the character of a *law of nations*. But still these principles will be *judicially* known to have had that character, up to the period of such legislative act; and the tribunal would still recognize them as being, in the absence of legislation, the best exponent of the will of the sovereign power.

---

[1] It will be shown, however, in subsequent chapters, that there are cases, incident to the settlement of new countries, or the establishment of laws in countries which have not before had a local, territorial, or national law, wherein universal jurisprudence —the *law of nations*, becomes practically operative in a more direct manner; that is, where it is not merely a judicial means of ascertaining what principles of the *local* law have universal personal extent.

And here appears the connexion or identity of the *law of nations* —universal jurisprudence—with the only *natural* law, having the character of a rule of action, which can in the jurisprudence of any one country be distinguished from the rest of the positive law.¹ Ordinarily, the *law of nations* of the period is always incorporated in the customary municipal (national) law of the forum,² operating either as internal or as international law; and such is the intimate connection of the two attributions of universality under a *judicial* discrimination of the law (*ante* § 29–36,) that it would be difficult to separate them. The instances will be few, if any there can be, where an opposition will occur of the *law of nations*, judicially cognizable at any particular period, and a local law having universal personal extent by judicial recognition only. Though it is plain that the supreme legislative power of the state may always disallow the rules of this universal jurisprudence by promulgating a contrary rule, having either a limited or a universal personal extent within its own jurisdiction.²

§ 101. General or universal jurisprudence—the science of universal law, or the *law of nations*, so far as it exists distinct from the common or unwritten law of any one state or nation, is known by the long continued international comparison of the laws of various states; the ascertained harmony of their legislation, and of the judicial decisions of their tribunals; collected, digested and expounded by private jurists, and, in course of time, forming a distinct repository of legal principles, and, in some sense, a code of law having universal jurisdiction.³

---

[1] Hence the *jus gentium* of the Roman jurists was often described by them as being identical with the unalterable rules of natural justice. Inst. Lib. i. Tit. 2. § 11, and hence with the Roman rhetorical writers it is often identified with *natura, jus naturale*. See Savigny: Heut. R. R, B. i. c. 3, § 22, and compare *ante* § 19, 34; and Austin. Prov. of Jurisp. p. 190.

[2] Savigny: Heut. R. R., B. i. c. 3, § 22.

[3] Wheaton, International law, § 10, thus cites from Heffter's Europäischer Völkerrecht, § 2.

"According to Heffter, one of the most recent and distinguished public jurists of Germany,—'the law of nations, *jus gentium*, in its most ancient and extensive acceptation, as established by the Roman jurisprudence, is a law (Recht) founded upon the general usage and tacit consent of nations. This law is applied, not merely to regulate the mutual relations of states, but also of individuals, so far as concerns their respective rights and duties, having every where the same character and the same effect, and the origin and peculiar form of which are not derived from the positive institution of any particular state.' According to this writer the *jus gentium* consists of two distinct branches.

The distinction of the laws of any one state into rules which its tribunals are to extend to its domiciled subjects only, (or rather to persons who have never actually sustained relations under other laws,) and rules which, as having that universal personal extent which has been above described, they are to apply to all natural persons, whether they have or have not sustained relations under other laws, is necessarily connected with the recognition of such a general or universal jurisprudence—the science of a *law of nations* historically known by the application of international law. For the juridical and legislative action of nations or political states, is, as before shown, one of the most authoritative indices of natural reason, and therefore a test to determine what principles, in the local or internal law, may be judicially taken to be the effects of rules which are not only jural in and for that jurisdiction, but rules so far founded on the nature of man, in civil society, that they may be always judicially presumed consonant with the natural conditions of human existence, and therefore of universal personal extent or application;[1] and at the same time the separate judgment of

---

"1. Human rights in general, and those private relations which sovereign states recognize in respect to individuals, not subject to their authority.

"2. The direct relations existing between those states themselves.

"'In the modern world, this later branch has exclusively received the denomination of law of nations, Völkerrecht, Droit des Gens, Jus Gentium. It may more properly be called external public law, to distinguish it from the internal public law of a particular state. The first part of the ancient *jus gentium* has become confounded with the municipal laws of each particular nation, without, at the same time, losing its original and essential character. This part of the science concerns, exclusively, certain rights of men in general, and those private relations which are considered as being under the protection of nations. It has usually been treated of under the denomination of private international law.'

"Heffter does not admit the term international law, (droit international,) lately introduced and generally adopted by the most recent writers; according to him, this term does not sufficiently express the idea of *jus gentium* of the Roman jurisconsults. He considers the law of nations as a law common to all mankind, and which no people can refuse to acknowledge, and the protection of which may be claimed by all states. He places the foundation of the law on the incontestable principle that wherever there is a society, there must be a law obligatory on its members; and he thence deduces the consequence that there must likewise be for the great society of nations an analogous law." But compare *ante* § 37 and the note.

[1] Savigny, Vocation for our Age for Legislation and Jurisprudence, Hayward's transl. p. 110.

" On this point the well known prize question of 1788 merits consideration; which required a manual in two parts, of which the first was to contain a law of nature abstracted from the code. [*Code of Prussia,*] the second, an abstract of the positive law itself. This notion of the law of nature was very superciliously received, and thereby injustice was done to it; certainly, under this name, that ought to have been set forth which the legislator himself regards as universal, and not of mere positive enactment, in

each nation upon this point cannot, as has been shown, be manifested, except in the application of international law. In the present advanced state of jurisprudence, among civilized nations, when the various effects of international intercourse upon the relations of private persons have been so frequently made the subject of judicial and legislative consideration, the customary laws of commerce and war furnish rules which will be judicially known as authoritative, in ordinary cases, until new legislation intervenes. And it is rarely the case that a tribunal can make an original discrimination of its own municipal (internal) law, as being either universal or particular in its extent or application to private persons, when deciding on the international allowance of the effects of foreign laws.

§ 102. But if it is necessary in any case to decide,—whether any rule or principle of its own municipal (internal) law is to be taken, independently of any exterior authority, or criterion, to be an assertion of a universal principle—one applying to all mankind, or, rather—one to be applied to all persons within the jurisdiction of the state in certain circumstances of natural condition, irrespectively of their national character or previous subjection to other laws,—the tribunal can have no other guide than the rules of ordinary reasoning applied to the mode in which the municipal (internal) law is asserted or promulgated in reference to persons and things within its own territorial

his laws;— an interesting historical problem; exactly resembling that of the Roman *jus gentium.*"

As will be shown hereafter, the Romans took the *jus gentium*, i. e. law known by its acceptance among all nations, to be the best exposition of the law of nature, regarded as a rule of action, or a *law* in the primary sense of the word. After the establishment of Christianity in Europe, the Christian Church assumed the possession of a criterion of the law of nations, in a Revelation of which it was the instrument and exponent. (Arnoldi Corvini Jus Canonicum, p. 2.) It then denied the authority of the natural reason of mankind, however concurrent; and in a large part of Europe—perhaps the whole of Europe, anterior to the reformation, the canon law took the place of the *jus gentium* of the Romans; that is, became the written code of universal jurisprudence. In the canon law digests, *natural law* is first asserted as that part of the national law of each country, quod inter omnes populos peræque custoditur: it being understood that the exposition of this universal natural law is the organized Christian Church. (T. Bozius, *De Jure Status.* Romæ, 1600.) From this time it would appear that jus gentium and law of nations, in the modern writers, were put for a law of which nations are the subjects, which law, as will hereinafter be shown, was, during the Roman Empire, identified with their *jus publicum* and *jus feciale.* Compare Decretals Prima Pars. Distinct. I. c. ix. Phillimore on International Law, p. 24, note. Heineccius, 1737. Jur. Nat. et Gent. L. I. c. i. § 21. Butler's Horæ Juridicæ Essay, Canon Law.

limits. It is probably impossible to state any legal rules controlling that judgment of the tribunal, (arbitrium boni viri,) unless equivalent to the following:—

1. If the will of the state, in reference to the action of private persons in certain supposed circumstances, is expressed by direct legislative acts—a form of words,—it may be expressed in words requiring a universal application, or an extent to all natural persons within the jurisdiction of the state.

2. Wherever the local internal law, derived either by positive legislation or by custom—judicial interpretation of natural reason, attributes rights or duties, to the native or domiciled inhabitants of its jurisdiction, as the incidents of a relation existing independently of the *rules of action* which it enforces as positive law; or, to vary the form of expression, where its rules of action are predicated upon the recognition of such a relation as being part of an existing state of things, in which such persons as the constituents of society are found, and as being the effect of law in the secondary sense of the word, (and therefore of *natural law*, in the only sense in which it is, in jurisprudence, distinguishable from positive law, *ante*, §§ 19, 57,) the source of that local law must be judicially presumed to attribute the same rights and duties to all persons within the jurisdiction or forum, who are in the same circumstances of natural condition.

§ 103. But since the supreme national power of the state may always, by special legislation, determine the legal relations of any particular persons within its domain, and legislation, where it exists, is superior to any indication of the will of the state judicially derived from any other source, the private international law of any one country may, in part, consist of rules applying to aliens (or persons anteriorly subject to other jurisdictions) only, thus derived from positive legislation, modifying, wherever they extend, the judicial application either of principles derived from universal jurisprudence—the historical *law of nations*—or of principles of the local law having before had a universal personal extent within that jurisdiction. So that private international law, as well as every other branch of positive law, may be ascribed either to a natural origin, or to a positive one strictly so called;—positive legislation.[1]

§ 104. The international law, in determining under judicial application the rights and duties of persons not sovereign, or not holding sovereign power, is thus a part of the private law prevailing within a national jurisdiction—a rule for persons and tribunals under that jurisdiction, coexistent with the private municipal or internal law therein, and distinct from it in its object and purpose, but not in its authority or political source. It being observed that by such a distinction in the object of the law, and by the recognition of persons as alien to the supposed municipal (internal) law, the first part of international law, (according to the division before given, § 48,) is necessarily implied; which part has the character of law in the secondary sense only, being axiomatic principles connected with the existence of states and nations, among which the three fundamental maxims before given, (§§ 63, 67, 68,) are in fact comprised. Thus the international private law, as well as every other branch of private law, has also the nature of public law, since it determines, to a certain extent, the mutual relations of states, or the holders of sovereign power. Though, so far as it may do this, the rights and duties of states, incident to those relations, are not the effect of *law* in the same sense as are the rights and duties of private persons, growing out of those relations; the international law being, for private persons, a law in the strict sense of the word, by the authority of the author and source of that municipal (national) law, to whose jurisdiction they may be subject; but, for states or sovereigns, only a law acknowledged by themselves to have moral obligation,—a rule of "positive morality."[2] It being only by way of analogy that any rules of action can be called a *law* for sovereign nationalities.

§ 105. The settlement, on general principles, of the international prevalence of laws having different national origins, forms that topic of jurisprudence which has been denominated by Huber, Story, and others, "the conflict of laws."[3] Strictly

---

[1] Compare *ante*, §§ 29—36. [2] See *ante*, § 11, and note.
[3] The phrase collisio legum (Hertius) is also employed: with the Germans—Collision der Gesetze. This, like the term *comity*, has been called by some of them a

speaking, there are no conflicting *laws* known to any national jurisdiction. Every rule which has the force of law within any one such jurisdiction derives its force from one sovereign will, and conflicts with no other rule having the same force; whatever may have been the process by which it is judicially ascertained or derived, either by following judicial criteria of natural reason, or the expressed will of the political source of law for that jurisdiction. This is a consequence of the first two of the three fundamental maxims before given, or only another mode of stating them.

§ 106. If the supreme power of the state maintains within its own domain any rights or obligations of persons which have not attached to those persons under its own territorial or local law, the law under which those rights and obligations were created has a particular personal extent, or operates as a personal law. The private international law is a personal law so far as it applies only to a certain class of persons, viz. aliens, or persons who sustain relations which have been created by the law of a foreign jurisdiction, (§ 53.) Those relations having been once thus recognized in international law, the rights and obligations arising from them will be continued, in the same territorial jurisdiction, when such aliens become domiciled inhabitants; unless there is some provision of the local (internal) law which specifically forbids their attribution to domiciled subjects. And the law which had at first a personal extent, by being internationally recognized in the case of aliens only, may thus thereafter become a part of the municipal (internal) law having a new territorial extent.

§ 107. It should be noted that the principle upon which this international recognition and continuance is made is not that the law recognized had a personal character, originally, in the territory in which it first existed, and established those rights and obligations which are here supposed to become the subject of

---

romantic—" abentheurlich "—expression: (Maurenbrecher: Deut. Pr. R., 2. Ausg., § 76, not. 3.) Wæchter, admitting that the term is liable to misconstruction, retains it because its significance is now well understood. Archiv. f. Civ. Prax. Bd., 24, p. 237, n.

As to the case of different laws originating under the same national authority and not conflicting in this sense; see Bowyer: Univ. Pub. Law, p. 146—7. Lindley's Thibaut, § 37. Savigny: Heut. R. R., B. III., c. i., §§ 346, 347, 348.

international recognition. All laws determine relations of persons, (*ante*, §§ 21, 22,) but, according to the view here given, the personal character of a law thus internationally supported is a consequence of its international recognition, rather than the cause of it. It is said by writers on the conflict of laws quoted by Story, in Confl. of Laws, p. 12, that "personal statutes are held to be of general obligation and force every where;" and these are contrasted with *real* statutes which are said to have no *extra*-territorial force or obligation. By *statutes* in that use of the term are not intended legislative enactments, but any rules of law affecting relations of persons to other persons and to things:[1] and by *personal statutes* are generally intended those rules which have determined the individual rights of private persons and their capacity for relative rights;[2] though the difficulty which has been experienced in stating general rules to distinguish what statutes are real, what personal, and what mixed, is a proof of the insufficiency of the distinction to determine their international admission.[3] It would, perhaps, be equally correct to say, that statutes which are held to be of general obligation and force every where are personal statutes. Their personal character would then be the result of the extent judicially given to them: and the question is—when will a judicial tribunal be bound to admit them to have this personal extent? If the authority for the tribunal, in doing this, is found in the historical fact of their international recognition, then their personal extent is, in fact, derived from the customary law of the forum.[4]

---

[1] Fœlix: Dr. Internat. Pr., § 5. "*Statutum*, coutume particulière." § 19, "Mais en même temps le terme *statut*, surtout dans la matière du conflict des lois est employé dans un sens plus étendu, et il est pris comme synonyme du mot *loi*." Merlin: Repertoire, *tit. Autorisation Maritale.* Bowyer: Univ. Pub. Law, p. 163. 2 Kent Comm., p. 456–7.

The term appears originally to have been used to designate a law whose territorial extent was limited to some several province or district of a national state or kingdom, and in that contrasted with the common law of the land. Savigny: Heut. R. R., B. III., c. i., § 347. Thus in England the particular customary laws of borough English, and gavelkind (*v.* 1 Bla. Comm., 74, 75) correspond to *statuts* of the French Provinces.

[2] Story's Confl. of Laws, § 51, and generally ch. iv. of that work.

[3] Reddie's Inq. in Internat. L., pp. 425—7. Hertius: De Collisione Legum, § 4, speaking of real, personal, and mixed statutes:—"verum in iis definiendis mirum est quam sudant doctores."

[4] Schæffner, § 31. Reddie's Inq. in Internat. L. pp. 477–8. Various European writers for and against this view are cited by Wæchter in Archiv. &c., Bd. 24, pp. 255—261.

It would indeed seem, from the writings of the civilians, that there was a period in the jurisprudence of Continental Europe when this personal character of a law was regarded as the juridical basis of the international recognition. And it is plain that after laws of a certain class or character,—laws affecting a specific class of relations,—have, in a number of instances, been allowed international recognition on other grounds, the fact of their having been admitted to have a personal extent within foreign jurisdictions becomes an evidence, to the tribunals of any one *forum*, of their jural character; and, by that international recognition, they may have acquired that historical universality, which gives them, before the individual judicial tribunal, a legal existence distinct from the municipal (internal) law—the law having territorial extent in and for the forum of jurisdiction. As a class of laws which have received international recognition, in determining the relations of persons passing from one territorial jurisdiction to another, they may be called *personal laws*, and so distinguished from laws which have had extent only within certain territorial limits.[1]

Most of the cases, also, which are cited by writers on this subject, to show the international recognition of certain laws denominated *personal* laws, have arisen between jurisdictions which, though having distinct local laws, were under one sovereignty or supreme political power: wherein, therefore, the laws of each province would necessarily be regarded as jural by the tribunals of other provinces under the same sovereign: as in the different provinces of France, when different local laws prevailed therein, but all deriving their legal force from a single juridical and legislative authority.[2]

§ 108. The various legal relations which a person may sustain, in respect to persons and things, together constitute his legal condition. Some of the rights arising out of those relations must, in their nature, be local, and can be exercised only

---

[1] Some states, though correlatively independent, may still be so connected by a customary international law, that laws affecting the condition of their respective inhabitants have a reciprocal recognition in their several tribunals which is not given by those tribunals to laws particularly derived from other states. As, for example, the various dominions constituting modern Germany. Comp. Savigny: Heut. R. R., B. III., c. i., § 348. Wæchter: Archiv. f. d. Civil. Pr., Bd. 24, p. 252.

[2] Pothier: Coutumes d'Orleans, ch. i. Fœlix: Droit Internat. Pr., p. 24.

in the jurisdiction wherein they were first created, (*ante*, § 75.) But the individual and also the relative rights of a legal person, if considered without reference to any specific *things*, may (irrespectively of their political guarantees,) continue the same in different national jurisdictions, and be considered continuing incidents of his personal condition. In a vague use of the words, such rights are often denominated *personal rights*. When the personal condition of a private person is spoken of, or a law is termed a law *of condition*, the term has reference more especially to the possession of such rights. In the Roman law, the rights which might be attributed to private persons were classified as rights belonging to different conditions, known under the name of *caput* or *status;* some rights being recognized independently of local laws, as being founded on a universal jurisprudence or *jus gentium*, and others being limited to the inhabitants of certain localities, being ascribed to the *jus proprium*, or *civile, Romanum*.[1]

§ 109. If, then, by the private international law which obtains in some one national jurisdiction, (either from positive legislation, or by judicial application of natural reason,) some relations of alien persons may be recognized and enforced therein which have existed under the law of a foreign jurisdiction, it will be remembered, according to what was said of the distinction between persons and things in the first chapter, that a legal relation can have that character only by a recognition of legal persons, and their capacity for legal rights. A contract, if internationally recognized as the effect of a foreign law, is necessarily known to the judicial tribunal through a recognition of a capacity to contract in some natural person. The law of the capacity of natural persons for legal relations, as the law of personal condition or *status*, must, therefore, enter into the international recognition of municipal laws supporting contracts. This capacity of persons is also an object of legal recognition in other relations of persons which do not have the character of contracts: some of which relations are recognized in different national jurisdictions as having a foundation in universal jurisprudence—the historical *law of nations:* such as the relations

[1] See *ante*, §§ 18, 19, and §§ 96, 97.

of parent and child, husband and wife, guardian and ward. These relations have a legal existence in all national jurisdictions by force of customary law, having the character of principles of universal jurisprudence: although different systems of municipal (internal) law may differ in their recognition of the inception of those relations, and even differ in their judgment of the combined rights and obligations arising from them.

The law of legal capacity and personality lies, therefore, at the foundation of private international law, as well as at that of the private municipal law, received or existing in any one nation or state; and the relations of persons which, together with distinctions of capacity, constitute freedom or liberty, and slavery or bondage, may be a topic of international private law, applied in any national jurisdiction, as well as of the municipal (internal) private law prevailing therein.[1]

§ 110. It appears, therefore, that when it is attempted to apply the general principles, herein before stated, in questions of the international recognition of those reciprocal rights and obligations which, in relations between private persons, constitute a condition of freedom or its opposite, the first principle which will apply is, that—

When persons appear within any particular national jurisdiction who have, by the law of a previous domicil, held such rights or sustained such obligations, the conditions of such persons, in respect to those rights and obligations, will be recognized, allowed, sustained, or continued by the judicial tribunals of the new forum in which they so appear, (unless legislation intervene,) when the relations constituting that condition are founded on principles which have, in the history of jurisprudence the character of universality, or of being part of a *law of nations:* because, as has been shown, this historical *law of nations*—these principles of a universal jurisprudence—may be judicially received to indicate what relations are consistent with that measure of justice which the state intends to apply: though they are always liable to be disallowed, within the jurisdiction of each state, by its own autonomic legislative and juridical

---

[1] *Ante,* §§ 25—27, and §§ 53, 54.

action, and so, in that jurisdiction, to lose their antecedent authority, as guides for the judicial action of a tribunal.

This *law of nations* may include principles determining the possession of either individual rights or of relative rights, and may thus operate as a law of *status* or *personal condition;* which, by its general recognition among different nations, would then have a personal extent, both in international and municipal (internal) law.[1]

§ 111. By the same authority from which every principle of this *law of nations* is derived, i. e., the concurrent juridical action of different states in international relations, some principles of this *law of nations*, determining the condition or *status* of private persons, might be exclusively applied to a distinct class, or definite portion, of mankind: and they would then have a peculiarly personal extent and character, whether manifested in international or municipal law: being, in such case, a law not only of personal condition, but a law of, or for, certain persons only: though being also properly attributed to universal jurisprudence—the law of nations—from their actual historical recognition among all nations.[2]

§ 112. A condition, or *status*, which should consist simply in the possession, or non-possession of individual or absolute rights, may easily be supposed to continue the same after a change from one jurisdiction to another. Those elements of condition which arise out of the relations of *family*—of husband and wife, of parent and child, of guardian and ward—may also be the same, in their essential features, after such a change.

The name of *bondage*, or *servitude*, may, as has been stated in the first chapter, be attributed to various conditions of obligation in private persons, even when the rights correlative to such obligation are rights of other private persons only;—not of the state, or some possessor of political power, (*ante,* § 47.) When spoken of as the condition of a *legal person*, the obligations in which it consists may exist in reference to persons and things peculiar to some one place, or jurisdiction; or, it may be

---

[1] In connection with this section see particularly *ante,* §§ 99, 100.
[2] See *ante,* §§ 53, 58.

said, the relations of which it is an incident may have an essentially local character; being such as could not be upheld, or continued, except in and for some jurisdiction by whose local law they were created. The relation of master and servant, when consisting in the involuntary absolute servitude of one person in respect to all objects of action—correlative to the right of another private person, is one which might continue the same in any jurisdiction. Whenever the servitude is limited, and in reference to specific local personalities things or circumstances, it is a condition which cannot exist in other states, or national jurisdictions, to which the subject of that condition may be transferred. Such a condition of bondage cannot, therefore, become one recognized by *universal jurisprudence*, or *a law of nations*. Absolute servitude of a legal person, in respect to all objects of action, might, however, be so recognized under principles having that historical character. Still more easily may *chattel* slavery be so recognized; it being a condition which in every state may be the same; for a thing—the object of rights, may be such within any territorial jurisdiction.[1]

§ 113. Whatever incidents in the personal condition of an alien should be ascribed to universal jurisprudence, by the tribunals of any one national jurisdiction, would be sustained, as under the *international* private law of the forum, while he should continue therein in alienage, and would become recognized effects of the municipal (*internal*) private law on his acquiring a domicil; taking effect as a personal law, (*ante*, § 54.) In other words, the rule of action, to which those incidents should be ascribed, would have like operation in the *new forum* upon the condition of the person coming from another jurisdiction, whether he should, or should not acquire a domicil in the new forum. While considered an alien, the operation of such rule would be classified under international law; and upon his acquiring a domicil, the same rule would become a recognized part of the municipal (internal) law. In this case, there would be no *conflict* between the laws of different jurisdictions, and no illustration of the so-called rule of *comity*, (*ante*, § 96.)

§ 114. If any incident of the personal condition of the alien

[1] Compare §§ 44—47.

is not founded on, or supported by this universal jurisprudence, or historical *law of nations*, its support in the forum of jurisdiction is then dependent upon the principle of *comity*, or that principle (the reason and nature of which has been before explained, §§ 76–78,) which gives admission to the effects of foreign laws, so far as natural circumstances of condition admit therein of the continuous existence of relations which first arose under the law of the former domicil; and the foreign law, creating those rights and obligations, may receive a personal extent under the authority of the sovereign of the *new forum—the forum of jurisdiction*. But the operation either of the *law of nations*—universal jurisprudence—or of the judicial rule of comity, upon the condition of alien persons, may always be contravened by the autonomic legislation of the supreme power. And the legal effect of each is also constantly subject to the limitation of a judicial application of rules, identified with the local law, (the internal law,) having *universal personal* extent. For if the local law attributes any rights, or obligations, *universally* within its jurisdiction,—i. e., to all natural persons, or to all natural persons in certain circumstances of natural condition, the possession of which is inconsistent with the relations formerly sustained by such persons under the law of their previous domicil, then the rights and obligations which, in those relations, constituted conditions of freedom, or its opposites, cannot, according to the general principles before stated, (§§ 77, 88,) be judicially sustained, nor receive a personal and international extent, under the authority of the sovereign of the forum of jurisdiction, either by force of comity—the *judicial* rule—or by being the effects of rules which may antecedently have been actually common among all nations, or have acquired the historical character of a *law of nations*.

§ 115. In determining what principles affecting the condition of persons domiciled under the local law, (or, in other words, what principles of the *internal* law,) are to be taken to have this universal personal extent to all natural persons within the national jurisdiction, the most authoritative indication is in such statutory enactments as may give this extent to the attribution of any right. Next in order are judicial precedents of antecedent tribunals representing the same political source of law; though, from the manner in which the extent of any principle is judicially determined, such precedents are hardly distinguishable—separately from the customary recognition of universal jurisprudence, (see *ante*, §§ 99, 100.) In countries wherein jurisprudence has long been developed, the test of this universality of extent will ordinarily be found in one or the other of these sources of law—either the *law of nations*, or positive legislation. But if cases, affecting personal condition, are supposable in which these do not apply, it may be taken to be a legitimate result of the axiomatic principles of jurisprudence, rendered legally authoritative by the practice of legislating states, that wherever (in whatever national, or independent jurisdiction,) the juridical declaration of capacity for legal rights is not made by creating a relative condition of legal superiority for certain natural persons over other natural persons, but is judicially recognized as the statement of a law in the secondary sense of the word *law*, or of a mode of existence, antecedent to all rules of action embraced in the positive law of that jurisdiction, it has therein (in that jurisdiction) the character of a law of universal personal extent, which must be judicially applied as municipal (internal) law, and also as international law. Where, therefore, the local, or municipal law, operating as the internal, or territorial law, upon persons regarded as its native, or domiciled subjects, takes cognizance of them as legal persons, as well as natural persons, attributing to them capacity for legal rights and duties, simply as a part or incident of the attributes of natural persons, the constituents of society, it thereby declares, or recognizes a natural law or principle—a law in the secondary sense—which must be received and applied by its tribunals, or judicial officers, as a universal law in reference to natural persons appearing within its jurisdiction. And, in this case, no law of a foreign jurisdiction regarding a natural person as a *thing*, or *chattel*—the *object* of rights only, without capacity for rights—can be allowed by those tribunals to have international recognition; unless, by direct act of positive legislation, (statutes, or treaties,) such law of a foreign jurisdiction, formerly binding on the alien, is allowed to take effect as a law personal to him, and exceptional to the local, or territorial law. The alien must be regarded, in all judicial processes, like the native or domiciled inhabitants of the jurisdiction, as being possessed of all the rights which the local law attributes to natural persons who are not aliens, and as owing only those obligations which are derived from some law for *legal persons*, and of such a character that they may be recognized internationally without contravening in other respects the law of natural rights and universal application as judicially known in that jurisdiction.[1]

116. But personality or capacity for legal rights might be recognized in all natural persons by the laws of one national jurisdiction, though relations might also be established, under those laws, which would give to one person a control over another, such as is inconsistent with the legal possession of personal liberty by the latter; and these rights of control and correlative obligations of subjection might be internationally recognized in other national jurisdictions, as the incidents of a relation between *legal* persons. Thus the loss of personal liberty under the criminal law of another state might be internationally supported, while the personality of the individual whose freedom is compromised or denied is not disallowed. Or the relations of parent and child, guardian and ward, master and servant,—where the servitude of the latter is involuntary, though not of the *chattel* character,—might be internationally allowed in a jurisdiction wherein, on the grounds above stated, *chattel slavery* could be disallowed or ignored, under a judicial application of the private international law. But it is impossible to conceive of a legal attribution of personality without at the same time attributing some definite or specific legal rights, individual or relative (*ante* §§ 45, 46.) Whenever *legal* obligations are attributed to a natural person, the law, which creates those obligations, must enable him by a legal capacity for choice and action, to fulfil those obligations,—recognizing such action to be according to a legal faculty or power of action,—and consequently recognizing a certain possession of legal rights. It would otherwise enable others to act in reference to him simply

[1] See *ante*, § 102.

as an *object;* and so make him a chattel or thing, to which not even legal *obligations* can be attributed. Legal personality must consist in and by rights, (§§ 43, 44.) The municipal (local or internal) law must make this recognition of personality by the attribution of some rights; though it is not necessary, and is, indeed, naturally impossible, that all persons should sustain similar relations. Some rights, however, may be attributed to persons which are not incidents of relations of specific persons to other specific persons, or which may be equally attributed to any number of persons; while others must be taken to be incidents of relations caused by laws having, necessarily, limited personal extent, (§§ 55–57.) Where by the local or internal law all domiciled inhabitants are recognized as legal persons, irrespectively of the possession of *relative* rights, ordinarily so called, (§ 40,) and that recognition of legal personality is made, not simply as the attribution of a naked right to life, protected by public criminal law, vindicating the welfare of the state, (§ 45,) but by attributing definite *individual* or absolute rights, protected by the private law of remedy,—there the local law, attributing those rights, must be looked upon as the recognition of, or statement of, a law in the secondary sense,—a natural law; and those rights be taken to be the incidents of a state of things existing independently of rules of action established by the state. Being of this character it may be judicially taken to be a law of universal personal extent; that is, one applying to all persons within the power or recognized territorial jurisdiction of that law, and those rights may be attributed to all, as being natural or primordial rights,—that is, rights incident to the condition of persons in the simple primordial relation of individual members of civil society. Where the right of personal liberty is thus attributed by the municipal (internal) law to each individual domiciled within the limits of a state or national jurisdiction, it must be taken to be attributed to those natural persons under a law intended, by its political source, to be a law of universal personal application; which is to be judicially taken to apply to all persons within the territorial jurisdiction of that law, irrespectively of their domicil or their previous subjection to other laws or jurisdictions; and this attribution of that right

THE EFFECT ON STATES. 109

will be made whenever the condition of a person is to be determined under the private international law of that jurisdiction.[1]

§ 117. But where the local (internal) law itself supports relations, between its domiciled inhabitants, in which some persons do not enjoy the rights of personal liberty, or are placed in a condition of obligation, correlative to the rights of others, which may be called a condition or *status* of slavery or bondage,—there the local law does not attribute the right of personal freedom, nor any other right,—inconsistent with such condition of bondage,—universally, or to all natural persons. And, according to principles before stated, the slave or bond condition of an alien, caused by, or existing under the law of his former domicil, will receive judicial support, or become realized, actualized, or carried out under the " comity of nations " or the judicial rule which is known under that name : being then a legal effect ascribed to the private international law of the forum of juris-

---

[1] Though there may be a great want of harmony among the writers who, distinguishing between *real, personal* and *mixed* statutes, have attempted to give general rules for their international recognition, they have unquestionably agreed, to a very great extent, in saying that the *status*, condition or capacity for rights of a natural person is every where judicially determinable according to the law of his domicil. See Story : Conf. L. ch. iv. and the older authorities there cited. Savigny : Heut. R. R. B. III. c. i. § 362. Fœlix : Dr. Int. Pr. § 29.

This principle has been so often judicially applied that, subject to certain exceptions, more or less generally admitted, it may be regarded as a rule of the customary international private law of civilized states, having the character of a rule of *universal jurisprudence*. (See *ante* § 93.) But no one exception to this rule is more harmoniously recognized by the authorities than this,—that the condition of involuntary servitude established by the law of the domicil, will not be recognized in another independent territory wherein such a condition is unknown to the local law. See Story : Conf. L. § 96. Savigny : B. III. c. i. § 349 ; and § 365, A. 7. Wæchter : Archiv. Bd. 25, p. 172. Schæffner : § 34. Fœlix : Dr. Int. Pr. § 31, note. Phillimore : Internat. L. p. 335.

These authors, however, do not now explain how the tribunal is to know that the law which it has to determine and administer forbids, in this case, the operation of the general rule. They either state the exception as one founded on the customary international law of all states, or of a certain number of states, or of some one state, (making it a rule of some one national law,) or else they assume that the tribunal will derive it by a *subjective* conception of the will of the legislator or juridical sovereign. In other words, they assume that the tribunal must declare the existence of such a condition contrary to jural rules. In the first alternative it is evident that the customary international law, either of all states, or of a number of states, or of some one state, on this point, may be different at different times ; in the other, that it is the moral judgment of these writers themselves which makes the rule, and that it is an *a priori* assumption on their parts.

And there is another deficiency in this reference to the law of the domicil ; for since the domicil of a person is determined, in a great degree, by his own act of choice, (see Savigny : Heut. R. R., B. III. c. i. § 360, ¶ 2,) the question of domicil may depend upon the *status* ; for since a slave cannot, as such, elect a domicil, the question of his domicil may involve a prior determination of his *status*.

diction, that is, to a rule identified in its coercive authority with the rest of the municipal (national) law.[1]

§ 118. But though a condition of slavery or bondage may exist under the local (internal) law of the *forum* of jurisdiction, it may therein be considered accordant with natural reason in respect to certain specific local circumstances; being the effect of a law applying to a portion of the domiciled inhabitants in reference to the existence of those circumstances only, and having a peculiarly local or national character. And, notwithstanding the existence of this slavery or bondage, there may be, in the municipal (national) law of the same jurisdiction, a general or universal attribution of personal liberty and other rights inconsistent with the condition of the alien under the law of the foreign state, to all natural persons who are not in those peculiar circumstances of local character by which, or in reference to which, the slavery existing under the internal law is legalized, i. e. declared jural—consistent with natural reason. In this case the slavery of the alien could not be judicially supported on the ground of *comity*—the rule so called; because still contrary to principles having (with this recognized exception under the *internal* law) universal extent within that jurisdiction; even though the local slavery should constitute a *status* —a condition of rights and obligations—very similar in its social consequences to that existing under the foreign law.

§ 119. But though the bond condition of an alien should not be maintained and continued under the law of the forum of jurisdiction, because contrary to a universal attribution of personal freedom under the local law, it does not follow that that condition would not, under the juridical power of *the same forum*, be recognized to have been lawful in the place of his domicil—the foreign country. If, indeed, it is not a necessary consequence of fundamental principles, yet it has always been held, in the customary jurisprudence of every country, that the jural character or rightfulness of every effect of foreign law shall be admitted at least so far as that effect is confined to the national jurisdiction of that law; whatever may be the juridical opinion of other sources of law respecting such effect as the

---

[1] Compare *ante* § 68, note.

basis of rights and obligations to be enforced within their own jurisdictions. In other words, the relations or actions created or allowed by a foreign law are customarily recognized to have been rightful, in and for its own domain; even when rights and obligations incident to those relations or actions are not maintained or continued in the *forum of jurisdiction.* Therefore, although the right of an alien master in respect to his slave, sanctioned by, or existing under the foreign law—the law of their domicil—should be disallowed in the jurisdiction to which they are alien, yet, under a judicial application of natural reason, (that is, irrespectively of positive legislation,) it will be held to have been jural or rightful, as well as legal, in the foreign country—the domicil of such master and slave: or it will, at least, not be held to have been a violation of rights which in the *forum of jurisdiction* may be attributed to the slave, nor the subject of legal remedy in that forum.

§ 120. By the same reasoning it would appear that even where, under the *law of the forum,* the right of the alien master created by the law of their domicil would not continue, or be maintained as against the slave, yet rights and obligations existing under the latter law as between the master and third parties, in respect to the slave, would still be recognized and maintained. The validity of the master's right in and for the place of his foreign domicil being admitted, would lead to a judicial recognition of the obligations of third parties correlative to that right. The right of civil recompense for violation of his right as master, in the place of his domicil, might, therefore, be maintained against third parties in a jurisdiction wherein the relation itself, as between the master and slave, could not continue. So, too, contracts founded upon the ownership of slaves in foreign states would be judicially recognized, and the rights and obligations growing out of them be judicially maintained in jurisdictions wherein, under the private international law, the condition of slavery as between the alien owner and his chattel slave, or bondsman, could not continue.[1]

---

[1] But in some systems of municipal (national) law a character of immorality is ascribed to certain actions which prevents them from becoming, under the jurisdiction of those systems, the basis of legal rights and obligations; even though they may have created such rights and obligations in and for the foreign jurisdiction where such action took place. Compare Robinson *v.* Bland, 2 Burr., 1084.

§ 121. The operation of law upon the relations of private persons is a consequence of their being actually within the territorial dominion of the sovereign state or nation from whom that law proceeds. But, as has been stated, (§ 54,) those circumstances which, in international jurisprudence, are technically called *domicil*, determine in many cases whether the condition of a person shall be controlled directly by the law of the jurisdiction (the *internal* law) in which he is found, or, indirectly, by that of some other to which he may have formerly been subject. In many instances, the intention of the person to acquire a new domicil will be held to vary the legal nature of his relations both in respect to persons and in respect to things. Servants, or slaves, either with or without their masters or owners, may appear in a foreign jurisdiction, (a jurisdiction other than that of their domicil,) either as aliens seeking a new domicil therein, or as temporary inhabitants, still continuing, in view of the law *of the forum*, to have their former domicil. But, in a judicial application of natural reason to the condition of either of these classes of aliens, the principles which have been herein before stated are equally of force. Whenever by the operation of these principles, or by positive legislation, the slavery of an alien person is continued after a change of domicil, it becomes a result of the municipal (internal) law of the jurisdiction of which he becomes a domiciled subject. In the other case,—that is, when *the domicil* is not changed, it is, from the continuing alien character of the person, a result of the private international law of the same forum.

§ 122. It is always to be remembered that the international recognition of personal condition which has been considered in this chapter is only a *judicial* act, determined by general principles of jurisprudence, and that it is always subject both to the customary law on the subject (anterior judicial practice) which may have prevailed in the forum of jurisdiction, and also to the positive legislation of the sovereign of the forum, giving an original rule extending, or limiting, the entire judicial discretion of its tribunals.[1] The action of the state, or nation, being, as compared with the action of its tribunals, autonomic, or in

---

[1] Schæffner: § 31. Savigny: Heut. R. R., B. III., c. i., § 361 A.

dependent of law, in admitting or rejecting a foreign law upon the ground of comity, or in receiving or repudiating a principle before ascribed to the *law of nations*—universal jurisprudence.

NOTE.—In connection with the province of the judicial officer in this respect, a principle cannot be forgotten by American tribunals which is no where so fully illustrated as in the jurisprudence which they apply; but in stating which, in an elementary essay, it may be well to cite an authority of foreign origin. Waechter, in a note to the passage herein before cited, (§ 84, n,) after the words—" that the requisition of a constitutional form and the limits of constitutional power alone determine its validity "—i. e., validity of the statute—observes: (Tr.) " The determination of this must, unquestionably, appertain to the judge. That is to say—in our constitutional states—he is bound, in dispensing the law, to follow the legislative dispositions of the government only when they conform to the requisitions of the constitutional law. It is true that he is merely the servant and instrument of the law, (Rechtsgesetzes,) but, certainly, he is the servant of a *valid* law (Gesetzes) only. It is, therefore, both his province and his duty, before applying a rule which claims to be a law, or an exercise of the legislative function, to examine, according to the existing constitutional law, whether it *actually is a law*,—that is, whether it has those qualities which, according to the constitution, must belong to a valid law. If these are wanting, it is his duty *not* to regard the decree as a valid law. It is true that this has of late been denied by, &c., [citing a German writer.] But this opposite view would make the judge, in his function, the subject of the executive power, [that is, in a state where the executive and legislative functions are not clearly separated,] and destroy both his constitutional independence and the right of the citizen, which is, to owe a *constitutional* obedience, only, to the executive power," &c., &c. [Giving the German authorities.]

Printed in Dunstable, United Kingdom